SpringerBriefs in Law

AF788113

For further volumes:
http://www.springer.com/series/10164

Peter Hulsroj

The Principle of Proportionality

Springer

Peter Hulsroj
Hornbaek
Denmark

ISSN 2192-855X ISSN 2192-8568 (electronic)
ISBN 978-94-007-5774-5 ISBN 978-94-007-5775-2 (eBook)
DOI 10.1007/978-94-007-5775-2
Springer Dordrecht Heidelberg New York London

Library of Congress Control Number: 2012950380

© The Author(s) 2013
This work is subject to copyright. All rights are reserved by the Publisher, whether the whole or part of the material is concerned, specifically the rights of translation, reprinting, reuse of illustrations, recitation, broadcasting, reproduction on microfilms or in any other physical way, and transmission or information storage and retrieval, electronic adaptation, computer software, or by similar or dissimilar methodology now known or hereafter developed. Exempted from this legal reservation are brief excerpts in connection with reviews or scholarly analysis or material supplied specifically for the purpose of being entered and executed on a computer system, for exclusive use by the purchaser of the work. Duplication of this publication or parts thereof is permitted only under the provisions of the Copyright Law of the Publisher's location, in its current version, and permission for use must always be obtained from Springer. Permissions for use may be obtained through RightsLink at the Copyright Clearance Center. Violations are liable to prosecution under the respective Copyright Law.
The use of general descriptive names, registered names, trademarks, service marks, etc. in this publication does not imply, even in the absence of a specific statement, that such names are exempt from the relevant protective laws and regulations and therefore free for general use.
While the advice and information in this chapter are believed to be true and accurate at the date of publication, neither the authors nor the editors nor the publisher can accept any legal responsibility for any errors or omissions that may be made. The publisher makes no warranty, express or implied, with respect to the material contained herein.

Printed on acid-free paper

Springer is part of Springer Science+Business Media (www.springer.com)

Preface

I started to think about proportionality in a normative sense many years ago when I read about a US case where two Vietnam veterans had robbed a bank with great brutality, using semi-automatic weapons. The defence pleaded for acquittal, arguing that the actions had been a result of post-traumatic stress, caused by war-time experiences. The implication of the plea was supposedly that they should go free as they were not guilty in the normal sense of culpability. Detention in some institution for the criminally insane seemed not to be suggested. The defence failed, and yet for me the case put in the spotlight how society in criminal law is centred only on the relationship between state and accused, and tends to downplay the consequence of acquittal for possible future victims. Proportionality seemed partly wrongly anchored.

After a while I realised how much my thinking was generally influenced by proportionality and the attendant concept of symmetry. Thus I wrote an article, 'Three Sources—No River',[1] in which I attacked the idea in international law that what is not prohibited is allowed—the Lotus Case principle. I attacked this concept because it is logically wrong to assume that a negation of one solution automatically leads to an affirmation of its alternative. If this would be the case almost any suggestion could be upheld depending merely on how it would be presented procedurally. The idea of freedom in absence of proscription wrongly assumes that actions take place in a vacuum, and thus do not affect others. Yet, all actions or omissions have a wider effect, sometimes small, sometimes immense. Atmospheric testing of nuclear weapons on your territory is bad news for your neighbour, no matter how you present it.

My reflections on similar topics lead to other articles on the good neighbour principle and the addressees of human rights obligations[2] and have now lead to 'The Principle of Proportionality'.

Persons have anchors, just like proportionality, and I want to dedicate this book to my family, the most important anchor of all!!

---

[1] Austrian Journal of Public and International Law, 1999, 219.

[2] To the Rescue, All Hands: The Good Neighbour Principle in International Law, Irish Yearbook of International Law, 2006, 167.

Preface

Contents

Introduction

The purpose of the book that follows is to examine the province of proportionality. In a world of lip-service to logic we assume that what we do when designing society is generally guided by logic's eldest daughter, proportionality. We might not have explicitly labelled proportionality as a basic principle, yet we assume intuitively that it is a key ingredient when we construct society. An ambition of the seven largely self-standing chapters that follow is to show how wrong one can end up if dealing with proportionality in an intuitive way only.

A deliberate assessment of proportionality requires first of all an unambiguous definition of every element that might act as an 'anchor' of the proportionality, and thereafter a calibration of the weight to be allocated to each possible anchor, relative to the other relevant anchors.

Thus, when people complain that the salaries of corporate chief executive officers are disproportionally high what they are really saying is that the salaries are disproportionally high relative to the salaries of ordinary working stiffs. And this is undoubtedly true when the anchor is the salary of normal salary-men.

Defenders of the high salaries claim that the salaries are justified by commercial reality. Good CEOs can bring immense benefits to their companies and their salaries are proportional to expected benefit. Also this is often true. The disagreement is thus not really about proportionality, but about the anchor to which proportionality should be attached: the salaries of others or the potential benefit for the company.

In most countries the result of the competition between the two proportionalities is a compromise based on moral and political balancing. Seen in isolation the result might be argued to be disproportional because it does not reflect either of the two competing anchors completely, but in reality it is eminently proportional since the result is based on a careful weighing of several laudable societal goals, several competing proportionality anchors.

So, is all that we consider disproportional just a question of not seeing the proportionality anchor we prefer reflected in as prominent a way as we would have wanted? In many instances surely yes, but not in all. Real disproportionality exists!

When the rich world lets fellow humans in developing countries die from preventable starvation the stock-in-trade justification is that it is regrettable that their country could not save them. So there is an alleged proportionality that implies that the well-being of an individual is proportional first to his own wealth and thereafter to the wealth of his home country. Global wealth is not relevant, is not a conceivable proportionality anchor. Yet, most people and all Christians would agree that every life is of equal value no matter where it is lived, and everybody in the rich world worthy of the label 'human' would spend 100 dollars to save a life if he or she felt responsible in some kind of tangible fashion. In the final analysis this points to tangibility as a determining factor for our humanism—with sovereignty as a frequent de-sensitiviser, but one which can be overcome by friendship or kinship. We will be ready to spend 100 dollars to save a friend or family member even if he resides in another country. The topic of emotional proximity and the consequence for aid to the stricken is explored further in Chap. 3. What should be retained here is that no proportionality anchor can justify that some lives are treated as if of no value, particularly when they are lived against a backdrop of global prosperity. Disproportionality exists and can be terrifying.

But also proportionality anchors can be forgotten in the blazing light of competing anchors, or can be unduly downplayed because of the extraordinary gravitational pull of other factors. This, as well, is disproportionality and illustrations can be found in Chaps. 1 and 2, where examples from criminal law point to the blinkering caused by uncritical reception of conventional wisdom. When circumstances change, conventional wisdom often does not and that is a further part of the pathology described in Chaps. 1 and 2. However, it finds its most poignant expression in Chap. 7, where the point is made that Darwin's drivers of evolution will soon have run their course for the human species. With the imminent death of aspirational society where will the human being go? To which new anchors can we attach our proportionalities when a deeply ingrained paradigm changes?

Proportionality is the key building block of societal construction and hence absolutist thought is antithetical to true society. Absolutist regimes will tend to err because the various relevant proportionality anchors will not be represented by empowered advocates; the Tea Party is dangerous because it will tolerate no compromise with values other than its own. Categorical imperatives are intolerable simply because they are categorical.

When Robert Nozick takes an element of Kant's categorical imperative, the duty to always treat the human being as a subject, never as an object, and extends the logic to its ultimate logical consequence, you get a political theory which is beautiful, but absurd. Absurd because Kant's hypothesis is neither categorical nor imperative. A human being must always be both a subject and an object, and all that is imperative is that a balancing must be made between when he is a subject and when he is an object. When a human being is made an object to achieve an aim which benefits not only he himself it should be with the objective to build society, and the reality is that without such 'sacrifice' no society can be built. Nozick is ultimately prescribing anarchy in order to avoid that a human being must be treated as an object—but by doing so he obviously does not protect human dignity as he intends, he sacrifices it completely. More on Kantian thought and on Nozick's contortions can be found in Chaps. 1 and 4.

The cause of the various types of disproportionality described above is either ignorance or misconception. There is another type of disproportionality, however, and that is the wilful one. Every human being has experienced situations where he or she knowingly did things not supported by proportionality, simply because it was within his or her power and served utterly egotistical goals for which no possible objective justification could be found. Such disproportional actions we normally label as evil. We sometimes abandon proportionality knowing that it is wrong to do so. Very gross corruption rarely has a justification convincing even to the perpetrator. The argument that everybody does it might provide short-term relief for the practitioner, but obviously no substantive comfort. The conscience cannot be pacified, and hence must be suppressed.

Yet, it is a mistake to believe that evil is always an expression of the wilful sweeping aside of proportionality's imperative. We are trained to think that evil has both an objective and a subjective element, the objective one being that a protected good is lost, and the second one being that this loss is introduced knowingly. By maintaining the subjective element we perpetuate Christian morality, which has as its centrepiece that the mental state of the perpetrator is decisive. We are forced to look at the injurious situation from the perspective of the actor, not the victim. In Chap. 1 this is shown to be wrong albeit in a different context. But it is wrong also in the analysis of our perception of evil, mainly because by focusing on the subjective element we provide for easy absolution and downplay the adverse effect of actions on a victim who experiences the same loss whether the injury was caused deliberately or not.

In the law of torts responsibility is normally attached to whether an injury has been caused by intention or neglect, evil is not the parameter. Yet, even for torts the general rule is that responsibility only arises if the actor should have known better. Except for cases of no-fault responsibility, subjective culpability is still required to establish liability. It is, however, interesting that there is a trend towards increased application of no-fault and stringent liability in this field, mainly because of the availability of insurance. This move away from culpability stricto sensu signifies, in fact, an increased recognition of the victim's plight. It is perhaps a matter of personal judgment whether society should be heading towards universal no-fault liability, and therefore universal, all encompassing insurance, yet the pleasing effect would be that the victim, who is per definition always innocent, will always be compensated. Desired deterrence effects would not necessarily be lost by universal, all-encompassing insurance, since actors could still be held responsible against some sort of subjective requirement, like negligence, only their responsibility would be towards the insurance companies. The victim would always be compensated.

Be this as it may, the basic point about evil is about societal self-understanding and moral appreciation, even if these factors, of course, can shape also the legal system. When we believe that subjective guilt is decisive in determining whether something is evil we almost invite ourselves to close our eyes to unpleasant facts and to pin our hopes on the towering Christian doctrine of forgiveness.

Christianity's message of forgiveness has undoubtedly been a great civilising factor for the Occident, but has a downside in that its triumph has tended to allow a self-service approach to exculpation. Instead of earnestly seeking forgiveness from the ones we hurt, we now take forgiveness for granted or even replace the victim's forgiveness with our own. How easily we forgive ourselves! Morally this is, of course, objectionable, but even worse, self-service forgiveness tends to make us less attentive to avoiding causing injury.

Treating evil as objective is ultimately to adopt the victim's perspective and to enhance our perception of risk. Treating evil as objective strengthens our empathy and makes us less likely to seek own benefit at somebody else's possible expense. From a moral viewpoint it makes sense to make us lament the inopportune effects of our actions, even if, in truth, injury was caused only by bad luck—by the cruel statistics of a certain number of actions inevitably causing a certain number of injuries. When evil is objective our propensity to forgive ourselves, and therefore our willingness to take disproportionate risks, will diminish. We might end up acting less, but we will be acting more prudently.

What is more, our predisposition to associate evil with intent allows us to don the mantle of ignorance all too easily. Since we believe that real evil must involve a deliberate choice we build a comfort zone where the dictate of humanity and proportionality cannot reach us simply because we refuse to engage. A method to make us focus on the remedy for some of the worst kinds of this sort of arrogance is set out in Chap. 3.

Intellectual laziness is the biggest enemy of compassion. 'We are the World' concerts might once in a while shake us up, but why are they necessary? We know the misery, our eyes see, but we refuse to understand. If we as individuals and as a society really internalised that we are guilty, not only for the bad things we intend, but also for the bad things we allow, then we would reverse the course of inhumanity as it has ruled the world so cruelly since the start of society. Then we would no longer look the other way when Africa starves, we would leave behind the terrible heritage of having allowed the Holocaust, having allowed genocide in Rwanda, having allowed tragedy after tragedy, just because we did not really care!

In so many ways have we built a dehumanising society, with borders (Chaps. 3, 5), all manner of alleged categorical imperatives (Chaps. 1, 4) and views on crime that exculpate the largest ones (Chap. 6). It is the aspiration of all the chapters that follow to explain how a detached appreciation of proportionality can help shape better and more cohesive local and global communities!

It is not the aspiration of the book to provide a definitive definition of proportionality in a legal, ethical and societal sense. Others might strive to provide the Standard Model of Proportionality and that might have value, but in the present book a make-do concept of societal proportionality is used, namely one in which a human activity can be judged relative to a given value by assessing the degree of correspondence between phenomenon and value. Proportionality in this sense involves well-defined values as anchors, and scalability and balancing where different values compete. Proportionality in this sense shares heritage with the proportionality concept of the natural sciences, although outside natural sciences it cannot be completely mechanistic.

As little as the book can lay claim to absolute definitional wisdom, so little can the book aspire to identify all the areas where more rigorous application of the proportionality principle would be desirable. The more you gaze through this looking glass the more questionable cases you find. Hence, what the book tries to do is to show that even with a simple definition of proportionality you stumble over significant inadequacies in the way we have constructed society. The book invites remedy of the identified infelicities, and seek to inspire reflection on where we are going as a global community if we are serious about proportionality, and on what we can do to further improve. Proportionality is, of course, only one element of analysis. One can trawl through the design of society applying specified values, secular or religious, for instance, and new findings might arise, many of which might be useful. The basic point is that societal design requires deliberate analysis so that value judgments and embedded concepts are made explicit. This is particularly needed in democracy, because only by making assumptions clear will the citizen be in a position to make informed choices. When such deliberate analysis is done, proportionality in some form will always play a role!

[illegible]

Chapter 1
In Dubio Pro Reo

Abstract This chapter challenges the almost sacrosanct belief in in dubio pro reo, and explains how the interests of an accused must be traded-off against the interest of possible future innocent victims, if societal happiness optimisation is the goal of community. Divine justice is unachievable for human society, and letting the benefit of the doubt reign supreme in relation to likely recidivists leads to divine injustice towards future victims, who will have been denied the benefit of effective societal protection as a result.

Keywords *In dubio pro reo* • Beyond reasonable doubt • Benefit of the doubt • Risk balancing • Victims • Relativity • Happiness optimisation • Utilitarianism • Recidivism • Presumption of innocence • Proportionality

The theory of relativity was the most important breakthrough of the 20th century in the science of knowledge.

In philosophical terms, the relativity theory was anticipated by centuries of metaphysical thinking turning upon the question of how subjective reality relates to possible absolute truth. When this thinking matured into Hume's causation theory and Kant's denial of the possibility of intuiting things in themselves and his construction of an analytical system of gaining objective a priori knowledge, the science of knowledge had already firmly positioned itself on the path of understanding by virtue of relativity. Thus, all inductive and deductive logic operates on the assumption of relativity,[1] and relativity itself becomes an absolute truth, when required to establish absolute truth. When Nietzsche trumpeted moral relativity and Einstein ultimately the relativity of space, time and motion, our whole universe of understanding was engulfed by a heightened realization that things can only be understood when their interdependencies are understood. The colour red is relative

[1] *Reductio ad absurdum* constitutes a particularly twisted application of relativity, because relativity is used to show the invalidity of a certain line of relative reasoning. However, all paradoxes are ultimately failures of relativity or of its application.

P. Hulsroj, *The Principle of Proportionality*, SpringerBriefs in Law,
DOI: 10.1007/978-94-007-5775-2_1, © The Author(s) 2013

to yellow and blue, and comes into existence only when light is brought into relation with a reflective substance; it is intuited by humans only when the reflected light comes into contact with the human eye.

In this very broad sense of relativity, natural science operates on a non-discretionary principle. The concept of cause and effect, itself relativity, is predictable according to empirical laws, at least outside of quantum mechanics. When light hits a surface with a certain reflective quality, the colour red always results.

In the social sciences, cause and effect are not predefined by the laws of nature. Human society has the discretion to attribute an entirely nonsensical effect to a given cause. There is nothing stopping human society from making the wearing of red clothing an offense—even one punishable by death. We may argue that it is illogical or, if wearing red clothes is preserved for people who are over 2 m tall, we may argue that the punishment for a violation—the death penalty—is disproportionate to the crime. In both instances we are arguing from the perspective of relativity. In the first instance we are arguing that there should be no relation between wearing red and punishment (because there should be no crime) and in the second instance we are arguing that, even if it is despicable that short people wear red, the disgust that this may cause cannot be brought into a meaningful relationship with the death penalty.

In the social sciences, we therefore try to emulate the strict relativity of natural science, by attempting to ensure that we exercise our human discretion in such a way that social cause and social effect are in balance, are proportional. And, with a nod to Nietzsche, we accept that the balance we strive for is a product of our circumstances and of our times. Relativity squared in other words; the balance itself is relative and the connection between the balance and our circumstances and times is also relative.

The purpose of the following discourse is to investigate whether, in criminal law, we have acknowledged all relativities and associated proportionalities, and whether we have calibrated them in a fashion that would allow criminal law to claim common ancestry with the laws of the natural sciences.

Causal relativity is, in the first instance, not so much the issue. Over a long period, much thought has gone into the analysis of the social causes that should give rise to social disapproval. We are certainly not lacking in this, even if time and changed circumstances will continue to bring about changes in this domain. And also proportional relativity is well understood, when the issue is only what degree of social sanction should be attracted by a certain act of disapproved social behaviour.

Where we are terribly lacking is in acknowledging that crime is a triangular relationship between perpetrator, victim and sanction, or, more precisely, a quadratic relationship between perpetrator, victim, potential future victim and sanction.

Crime and punishment have their roots in perceptions of divine justice. And because divine justice is always a bilateral relationship between creator and sinner, it has been found natural to absolve the sinner of earthly disapproval if there is any doubt about his culpability.

In dubio pro reo is unquestioningly accepted as fundamental to the human perception of justice, although we inherently live in an unjust world, where some are born with extravagant ability and some with severe disability; some are born rich while millions are born to debilitating poverty, some are run over by a truck and others not.

Why is it then that an accused must walk, if there is any reasonable doubt about his guilt, even when probability shows that he is very likely guilty and that he is likely to repeat his crime? Utilitarianism would normally dictate that the possible pain caused to an innocent suspect should be weighed against the pain that will possibly be caused to a future victim, who is undoubtedly innocent. Yet even hard-line positivists like H.L.A. Hart, to whom utilitarianism should come naturally, shy away from accepting that someone likely to commit further crime, but still possibly innocent, should be condemned in order to seize the opportunity to avoid pain to an inherently innocent future victim.[2]

The arguments marshalled by Hart, and undoubtedly shared by many, are either moralistic or nonsensical. Hart's first line of argument is that society must value each individual as a person and therefore cannot impinge on the liberty of individuals without full proof of guilt. But one does not lead to the other, as Hart would normally be the first to point out. The trade-off is not between society and the accused, but between the liberty of the accused and the liberty of a potential future victim. Both are individuals and both have equal value.

Even if one believes in free will, and that culpability is determined by the exercise of free will in a disapproved fashion, it does not resolve the dilemma of the possible recidivist, because the potential victim does not have the free will to avoid becoming a victim. In moral terms, the dilemma is just restated to become a trade-off between respect for the free will of the accused against the lack of free will of the potential victim. The hallmark of a civilized society is that it protects the weak and it defies reason to believe that the accused is always the weak party.

In the past, *in dubio pro reo* might have served as a shield against the arbitrary decisions of kings and feudal lords, but in a modern society, where the exercise of public power is greatly circumscribed by other means, this function is less critical, even if it is still to be acknowledged as part of any value trade-off.

In an extraordinary display of twisted utilitarian logic, Hart argues that citizens should only be punished when they also experience the satisfaction associated with committing the crime. By only punishing people who are actually guilty of a crime society facilitates predictability, since citizens can plan the "cost" of their actions accordingly. As Dworkin has pointed out, this logic is obviously unsustainable, because if people thought about the issue in these terms they would not reach this conclusion.[3] Sadly, in the argument of a most detached and elegant philosopher, one hears the gentle echo of the crude emotionalism of New Hampshire's motto "Live free or die", because Hart does not, or will not, acknowledge that the

2 Punishment and responsibility, 158 ff.

3 Taking rights seriously.

price of avoidable crime is paid overwhelmingly by the victim. Hart's main thesis on the alleged inalienable rights of individuals is the one with traction—but, as discussed, wrongly so.

1.1 Where We Were and Where We Are

Evolutionary biology has had a remarkable ability to spread its "DNA" to other professional species; obviously to anthropology, but also a bit farther, to sociology, and much farther to political science and even negotiation theory. In fact, all behavioural sciences have been touched, with one notable exception—law. Now, law might be reluctant to be considered as a behavioural science, preferring to see itself as forming behaviour rather than merely studying it. This is a fundamental fallacy, however. Law obviously reflects social mores, and desirable behaviour is its *raison d'être*. Hence, it would be highly important to analyze law from the standpoint of evolutionary biology too, in order to establish law's correspondence with our behavioural ability as it might have been hard-coded through human evolution. One could then also question whether given legal norms would actually support the evolutionary goals of society, even if this smacks dangerously of "brave new world" and designing the superhuman. Yet, all educational systems and, in some implicit sense, all law, reflect evolutionary goal-setting by society. Alpha males don't like traffic lights.

Analysis of law from the perspective of evolutionary biology is basic science, which assists us in flushing out our most fundamental value judgments. In this vein, one may argue that the criminalization of polygamy is a rare, early example of female social interests being reflected in law. One may also argue crudely that the criminalization of polygamy reflects an evolutionary interest by making child-rearing more socially secure. But what was true at one stage of evolution is not necessarily true at the next. At a time when birth rates in the developed world are dropping dramatically, it would appear that making child-rearing more socially secure in this way is not doing the trick. Non-monogamous males avoid marriage and avoid the criminalization of simultaneous multiple partnering, but they also avoid the obligation to support the mother of their child during child-rearing, except for the limited financial obligation of paying child support. The prohibition of polygamy encourages serial monogamy, but not flexible family arrangements along the lines of the 1960s commune, although arguably, for one type of human being, the latter might be the better procreational vehicle. Without going too far into the subtleties of family law, the example of polygamy demonstrates the potential of evolutionary theory to differentiate value judgments embodied in legal norms. If the criminalization of polygamy originally served a procreational aim, then evolutionary theory shows that it serves this purpose no longer. The justification may then be sought in moral considerations, but in that case why then look only at the legal institution of marriage when multiple, simultaneous partnering is perfectly possible outside this legal institution, particularly in our day and age when life-long marriage is a rarity and so many seem to agree with Shelley's discrediting of monogamy:

I never was attached to that great sect,
Whose doctrine is, that each one should select
Out of the crowd a mistress or a friend,
And all the rest, though fair and wise, commend
To cold oblivion, though it is in the code
Of modern morals, and the beaten road
Which those poor slaves with weary footsteps tread,
Who travel to their home among the dead
By the broad highway of the world, and so
With one chained friend, perhaps a jealous foe,
The dreariest and the longest journey go.[4]

It would seem that biology has got the better of us, and that the criminalization of polygamy no longer truly narrows our choice. It only ensures that simultaneous partners cannot be granted the same legal protection as serial ones, and that may actually hinder procreation!

Looking now at evolutionary theory in relation to *in dubio pro reo*, it may be argued that this principle nurtures an indispensable human belief in free will and causality. It might be believed that our aspirational culture cannot survive without the belief that we are the creators of our own fortune, and that the conceptual corollary is that we will only be punished for the evil acts we have actually committed. Evolution has made us able to accept that we might be run down by a bus, but not that we may be punished by our fellow primates for something we did not do.

This is, however, demonstrably not so. Over the last couple of thousand years, humankind has experienced tribal blood revenge, feudal arbitrariness, collective punishment and genocide, leading any thinking person to the conclusion that human justice is often defective, and that there is little overlap between human and divine justice. Machiavelli cruelly demonstrated how the lives of individuals could (and, according to him, should) be sacrificed for some greater good, such as the prince's possession of his principality! *Pro reo* is often *in dubio*.

Against this view, it can be held that the greatest accomplishment of the Age of Enlightenment was placement of the rational individual at centre stage, ultimately resulting in the humanistic revolutions in France and America. These revolutions represented a paradigm shift from crude collectivity to democratic individuality, something that Americans seem to reinvent and re-appropriate with many a new president.

The collectivistic view of sacrificing possible individual innocence on the altar of prophylaxis might be considered antithetical to democratic individuality. In some sense, this might even be true. History is commonly seen as reflecting pendulum swings between conservatism and radicalism and, in the same fashion, there might also be pendulum swings between collectivism and individualism: a swing

[4] Epipsychidion.

from Adam Smith to Karl Marx and back to Adam Smith. Yet, every swing carries within it the seeds of its own destruction. Globalization is the epitome of individuality: anybody with capital can be a player in a borderless and virtually unconstrained world. The systemic imbalances in the world are the seeds that will either destroy globalization along the lines of the oil shock of the early 1970s or force communal action to correct the wealth imbalances, as national progressive taxation schemes did at the end of industrialization. The pendulum continues its swings between individuality and collectivity!

Aristotle famously spoke about the need to balance the appetites and this view has resonated throughout the ages, finding expression, for instance, in the psychology of Carl Jung and his views on counterbalancing natural tendencies—all a reflection of the desirability of avoiding the sharp edge of the swings of the pendulum.

As it happens abandoning full scale *in dubio pro reo* for the greater good exactly represents the Aristotelian balance of the appetites, rather than just a collectivistic extreme. The two appetites are for individual justice and for avoidance of innocent suffering. Striking a balance in which the benefit of the doubt is not invariably given to the suspected perpetrator but also sometimes, in a value trade-off, to the potential victim seems, in a roundabout fashion, to give ultimate effect to individuality and humanistic ideals.

A favourite activity of philosophers, starting with Hobbes, Rousseau and Locke, but also of present day incarnations such as John Rawls, has been to build castles in the air based on social contract theory. Society is seen as founded on original consent, or contract, and from this the great thinkers derive whatever conclusion fits their individual tastes. The field is open for everything from the misanthropy of Hobbes to the 1960s pop-socialism of Rawls. The concept is sometimes sanitized, for instance, by Rawls, who liked to imagine the social contract from a game-theory perspective, with the imagined original players not knowing which hand they would eventually have to play. They would have to construct their own social contract without knowing whether they would be intellectually privileged or not, whether they would be wealthy or poor, black or white, male or female. Although Rawls uses this device only to justify his own political preference, there is a kernel of relevance in this perspective, since there is no great leap from this view of social contract to the rational choice theories of economists. As mentioned above, Hart seems to believe that the rational choice of an individual would be unadulterated *in dubio pro reo*. However, in reality, the rational choice of individuals who are not criminals would have to be to sometimes sacrifice the purity and comfort of *in dubio pro reo* for the higher statistical chance of avoiding future injury: the result of a proper risk trade-off between the interests of a potential perpetrator and a potential victim. With a 90 % chance of repeat crime and 90 % certainty that a potential perpetrator is guilty, only a fool would choose *in dubio pro reo*!

You will have noticed that all of the above theories contain significant speculative elements, which, in some form or another, allow the subjective preferences of the discussant to be brought into play. The response of Aristotle to this scientific difficulty was empirical observation because, until quantum mechanics, it was assumed that observation did not influence results. Empiricism was therefore the solution that led to objectivity. By also seeking to apply scientific method to philosophy, Aristotle paved the way for utilitarianism, phenomenology and logical positivism.

Looking at our problem from the perspective of phenomenology or, even more concretely, from that of logical positivism, with its emphasis on provability, we may arrive at a conclusion which is, at least, unassailable in terms of cause and effect. Sociology without a political agenda!

Analyzing *in dubio pro reo* with the filter of cause and effect, it becomes clear that there are two causal chains to consider, each with its own set of problems. The first set of problems stems from the uncertainty about whether somebody accused of a crime can be safely assumed to be going to repeat the crime in the future, if indeed he was the perpetrator of the first crime. If there is no risk of repeat then there is every reason to let *in dubio pro reo* run its course, since the value of *in dubio in reo* in a concrete case overrides the general prophylactic benefit that could be gained by incarcerating somebody who is likely to be guilty, but not "guilty beyond reasonable doubt". Yet many criminalistic studies show that certain delicts committed by individuals of a certain type or in certain social circumstances will, with the highest degree of probability, be repeated when opportunity presents itself. Al Capone will run rum at any given chance. And certain sexual crimes have terrible records of recidivism. Hence, without delving into the realm of subjectivity, one can conclude that it is possible to assess the likelihood of repeat crime against an objectivised statistical database. Well-meaning criminologists often dispute this rather apparent fact, since putting the predictability of recidivism into question allows these experts to escape from facing head-on the moral dilemma arising. The dilemma is, of course, not only in relation to *in dubio pro reo*, but also in relation to sentencing and security detention, and it is as unacceptable to seek to avoid the issue by putting predictability into question as it is to avoid the torture debate by claiming that torture does not work, although demonstrably it sometimes does. Thus the *in dubio pro reo* debate must be had, and criminologists should in parallel increase the focus on creating ever sounder methods for the prediction of repeat crimes.

The second issue on causality is related to the solidity of the causal chain. When is the likelihood of guilt strong enough to carry a conclusion that prison should be ordained in order to avoid repetition? Logically, the less the likelihood of guilt, the greater the likelihood of repeat would have to be, or the more severe the crime. The issue becomes one of the balance between the likelihood of repeat versus the likelihood of innocence versus the gravity of the future offense. As a matter of principle, this is no more subjective than establishing whether somebody is guilty beyond reasonable doubt, despite the fact that in the latter case you work with only one variable and in the former case with three.

It is clear that viewing the matter in this fashion reflects a hardcore utilitarian approach. It is also clear that even if a utilitarian trade-off is conceptually objectivised, it also reflects a value judgment, namely that societal ethics must be as objective as possible. Without getting into the Bentham–Stuart Mill debate about whether there are qualitative differences in pleasure and pain, one must recognize that a large part of humanity operates on the assumption that ethics involve more than just optimizing pleasure. Many religious communities hold that human existence cannot be quantified in an object fashion. Escaping injury does not ensure a happy existence, and a happy existence may not even be the point of human existence. So doing right is not necessarily a question of doing the least damage. In terms of personal ethics, this is all highly respectable, but as a political theory it is both useless and entirely unethical. The objective of any political theory must be the maximization of happiness, because only then can one avoid imposing one's personal ethics on someone with potentially conflicting ethics. Separation of church and State is the banner slogan in this respect, and this separation allows a band of masochists to form a voluntary commune, in which they contractually agree that society's normal prohibition on flagellation does not apply. The society has maximized the happiness for everyone, and left those seeking fulfilment in pain to pursue their route. Freedom is only curtailed to minimize the pain of non-masochists.

In a curious way, there is actually an overlap between religious thought on self-sacrifice and loosening the rigors of *in dubio pro reo*. Although religious self-sacrifice should be voluntary, as explained above, the guiding principle—that one may have to sacrifice one's own interests in order to achieve higher aims—is exactly the same as the guiding principle involved in seeking to avoid repeat crimes through possible sacrifice of innocence. You may be incarcerated, although innocent, in the pursuit of the higher aim of avoiding harm to undoubtedly innocent citizens. The inversion of Hart's logic!

1.2 Proportionality from the Evolutionary or the Personal Perspective

When you start to think about proportionality you find it everywhere—in the disproportionality of Picasso,[5] the parameter-playing of Salvador Dali, the twelve-tone music of Schoenberg, the pseudo-realistic attempt to transfer thought processes to paper in the stream of consciousness of Ulysses. You start to wonder whether Einstein's work has made proportionality a platitude.

Yet, platitude or not, the fact is that the principle of proportionality has not become the dominant force in the social sciences in the way it has in almost every other walk of life. This is curious, because evolutionists would argue that proportionality is the root of life.

[5] You only really understand the distortions of Picasso if you take to heart his explanation of disproportionality as a result of visual priority, i.e. if you look at someone's eye, your focus on the eye will mean that the eye is magnified relative to the brow.

The activity in the primeval soup that ultimately led to life was predicated on proportionality. When the building blocks of life, under the influence of dynamic forces, started to form organized material structures, evolutionists preach that this was inevitable because the determining factor for propagation was effectiveness. Of course, nothing other than proportionality at play. Material organises itself relative to the dynamic forces that influence it. As life forms become more and more sophisticated, the relativity element becomes more and more evident. When evolution decides whether elephants shall have large or small ears, the determinant factor is the relationship between the entity "elephant" and the dynamic forces of influence—its immediate environment. As environments are different in Africa and India, relativity and evolution lead to different sized ears in African and Indian elephants.

Evolution might, however, lead to different characteristics living side-by-side, which means that relativity is three-dimensional. Relative to the same dynamic forces, a species might develop alternative survival strategies, and these might co-exist, because the relationship between the subspecies means that neither becomes completely dominant. Large seagulls might co-exist with smaller types, if this means that access to nutrition is optimized across the board. Efficiency factors ultimately determine the proportion of large and smaller sub-species—in the same way as the distribution of work between rats and mice determines the relative numbers of the two species.

Some evolutionists speak of evolutionary stable strategies to describe how equilibrium is ultimately arrived at between species or between subspecies. But evolutionary stable strategies are then merely a conceptualization of the triangular or, more accurately, multi-angular, relationship of subspecies, species and their dynamic environment. All a question of proportionality!

Dawkins suggests that the world and all its inhabitants are trapped in this proportionality.[6] Accordingly, all social organization is determined by the reaction of each individual (as a function of ever-competing genes, according to Dawkins) to his dynamic environment and to all other living beings.

If one puts on the cloak of an evolutionist one must then be astounded that social sciences, as pure phenomenology of evolution, have remained so uninformed of its dominant force: proportionality.

Neighbouring disciplines, such as economics, have subliminally embraced the principle of proportionality to a sometimes astounding degree. Financial instruments such as SWAPS, where interest obligations are exchanged to fit different risk and cash-flow profiles, are numerical expressions of proportionality considerations, with interest obligations becoming entirely dissociated from the underlying substantive obligations.

Game-theory models in economics are becoming entirely mathematical, involving a large number of variables, which, of course, are ultimately only expressions of proportionality—just like all mathematics and hence all quantitative economics. No variable exists without proportionality.

---

[6] The selfish gene.

For the purposes of our *in dubio pro reo* investigation, the aspects of economics and finance dealing with risk trade-offs are of greater interest, however.

Robert Rubin, wrote interestingly about how, as a former head of arbitrage at Goldman Sachs, he had risk-balancing as second nature, and one gets the impression that such cool calculation of risk was an almost unknown science in the Washington he encountered.[7] Of course, politics does deal with risk-balancing in terms of human relationships—between law-makers and the President, or between politicians and constituencies—but it is not used consistently as a tool for formulation of substantive policy. Many fundamental issues are not addressed, or are not even thought of as addressable, because the consideration of proportionality by politicians is skewed towards the appearance of good, rather than actual good. And this is never more obvious than when the short-term bad is necessary for the long-term good. The potential in the world for violent uprising feeds off the inherent "short-termism" of our kind of democracy.

If, however, we approach *in dubio pro reo* from the viewpoint of the arbitrageur's risk trade-off, we see interesting phenomena. We see that H.L.A. Hart was on to something when he tried to analyze the problem from the perspective of the individual. It is, indeed, right to adopt the grass-roots perspective, yet it has to be the grass-roots perspective of risk-balancing, not the perspective of whether an accused person has had "bang for his buck".

When not socially conditioned to think about the issue in absolutes, a non-criminal would naturally opt for some relativity in terms of the presumption of innocence, and put it in relation to the likelihood of averting future crimes. Applying the "original position" theory of Rawls, not to inflate concepts as he does but as a way of expressing the fundamental uncertainty about whether one would hold the potential victim card or the potential innocently accused card, the non-criminal will always want to accept a small risk of being condemned when innocent in order to have the opportunity to avoid becoming a victim.

Perhaps surprisingly, even some potential criminals would, in certain circumstances, prefer a toning down of the force of *in dubio pro reo*.

Perhaps a well-intentioned businessman in a corrupt country would prefer that corrupt practices could not be hidden behind *in dubio pro reo*, rather than being forced into the same corrupt practices in order to protect his livelihood. The price he would have had to pay would have been the risk of being innocently condemned, but that is a small price to pay compared to being forced to become a criminal oneself.

An even more striking example is crime in the slum tenements of the big cities in the US. *In dubio pro reo* protects the hoods, the drug dealers and the murderers. If they want to survive, children in tenements will see little alternative to becoming criminals themselves. Cleaning up tenements with a broad brush would inevitably mean that some suspicious innocents would be jailed. Yet, from the "original

[7] In an uncertain world.

position" of Rawls, the would-be criminal should opt for this negative risk in order to escape his deadly vicious circle.

1.3 The Inhumanity of Words

The 20th century was a highpoint in the search to understand how language structures logic and feelings and how logic and feelings structure language. Without getting into the subtleties of language theory, one must acknowledge that words have an inherent and potentially dangerous tendency to declare independence from the substance they were originally intended to describe. Epistemology is much about sweeping away the veils with which words shroud meaning.

A proper understanding of risk-balancing in criminal law has been hindered by exactly this propensity of language to allow unallowable shortcuts in logic.

One splendid example of this was the 2006 judgment of the German Constitutional Court, in which legislation allowing the downing of aircraft carrying innocent passengers in a 9/11 scenario was struck down as being in conflict with the German Constitution.

The wording of the German Constitution is emphatic in its protection of human life and dignity. With its painful history, it is also natural that Germany would be particularly concerned about the use of military force to down an aircraft carrying innocent passengers. Yet the judgment of the Constitutional Court, while well argued and relevant in many respects, errs badly in a central section dealing with the right of individuals to be treated as subjects rather than objects.

Constructing a central argument based on a distinction between subject and object is a betrayal of Germany's proud philosophical tradition, and is even grammatically incorrect under the rigid rules of German grammar, where the State, in the constellation dealt with by the Constitutional Court, will always be the subject and the citizen the object; the only question being, perhaps, whether it is the accusative or the dative object. Choosing between lives based on a distinction between an accusative and dative object, or an object and a subject, is obviously absurd linguistic hypostasis. This has nothing to do with Wittgenstein's and Derrida's chasing of linguistic ghosts and even overlooks that by recognizing the innocent lives in the aircraft as subjects, the court in its own twisted logic makes objects of the innocent lives on the ground.

How far astray one can be lead by founding theory on a distinction between the human as subject or object is illustrated by Robert Nozick's ultra-libertarianism,[8] according to which virtually every societal constraint on individuals constitutes a breach of their right to be treated as subjects rather than objects. Taxation is oppression and, for instance, the establishment of a public health system funded

[8] Anarchy, state, and utopia.

by taxes hence unallowable. Letting people die on the streets becomes moral, because every man is an island—a subject, and no obligation to help can be imposed. The common ancestry with Kant's categorical imperative, which Nozick claims for his logic, is absurd, even if Kant, indeed, as part of a humanistic ideal showcased the need to treat each individual as a subject rather than an object. But Kant would surely never have thought it part of a humanistic ideal to confuse the competing claims of subjects with the categorization of one as subject and one as object.

The central distinction made by the Constitutional Court is, in the final analysis, between the State as an active taker of lives and the State as a passive allower of the taking of lives. The Constitutional Court thus dives headfirst into the ethical misunderstanding that active evil is worse than passive evil. Admittedly, in adopting this view, the Constitutional Court is in good company, since criminal systems generally operate on this distinction. Yet, if the purported aim of the Constitutional Court is to give full effect to the requirement of the constitution to protect the lives and dignity of citizens, then compliance is measured in terms of results, not in terms of whether the State is active or passive. Using the court's own logic, the citizen becomes the object rather than the subject as soon as elements other than optimization of life and dignity become decisive. To distinguish between active or passive destruction of life by the State is to close one's eyes to results, and the Constitutional Court argumentation is in reality, based on its own premises, unconstitutional.

The various lines of argument used by the Constitutional Court could be replayed in exactly the same form when discussing *in dubio pro reo*. The touchy-feely statement on the individual as a subject rather than an object sounds as pleasing in this context, but it is equally wrong and for exactly the same reasons. Respect for the lives and dignity of citizens requires result orientation, be it in trying to avert 9/11 disasters or in trying to avert other crimes. And the whole point of relaxing the strictures of *in dubio in reo*, or of allowing the downing of aircraft, is to maximize the common good and therefore provide the best possible result in terms of the respect for life and dignity.

1.4 The Inner Human Needs

The endlessness of the universe, the seeming insignificance of individual life and the terrifying sense of being subject to laws of nature that are uncaring and not focused on individuals are the catalysts of the human quest for meaning. When our self-centred universe is confronted by the reality of the universe at large we seek ways, not necessarily to reconcile the personal universe with the physical universe, but to make sense of our personal universe as distinct from the physical universe. Religion demonstrates to us that there is a bilateral relationship between the individual universe and all the rest, between Me and God. By operating on the bilateral plane, the importance of every individual becomes comprehensible, because there is no need or invitation to add up the billions of bilateral relationships with the one God.

As an outgrowth of this way of thinking, *in dubio pro reo* seeks to equate earthly and divine bilateral justice, by seeking to ensure that only the truly guilty are punished. At least from a Christian perspective, this attempted equation is curious, however. The central message of the martyrdom of Christ is, indeed, one that concerns the strongest of bilateral relationships, that of father and son. But the son, although innocent, dies whilst under the authority of the father—he dies for others and is allowed to die for others. This message of sacrifice and self-sacrifice has been appropriated in many ways; it has often been misunderstood, has given rise to religious and secular cults of sadism and masochism and has fostered terrible cultures of servitude. It has, however, never been understood as an indictment of *in dubio pro reo*. The reason for this is, in a sense, laudable. As mentioned earlier, *in dubio pro reo* was originally also seen as a defence against the arbitrary exercise of feudal or pre-feudal power. In this, the principle served humankind well. Yet, with the advent of other ways to circumscribe the arbitrary exercise of power, the original ethical question must be re-examined. In this re-examination, the Christian bilateral message of unquestioning filial love is supplanted by the equally valid message of brotherly love. The message becomes one of potential self-sacrifice to preserve the well-being of others. A message, in fact, of readiness to endure not only physical adversity in order to serve others, but also to endure infamy in doing so. The Bible is full of examples of indignities suffered for the faith, the epitome of this being Christ, who not only died for others but who was crucified as a common criminal. This parallel must be borne in mind when we look at how the risk-balancing is to be done. Being put in jail when innocent not only deprives you of your freedom but also of your dignity. Both are cost features that must be outweighed by the benefits of damage avoidance.

Peter Strawson, in a twist on Voltaire's statement on the possible need to invent God, has said that humans need to believe that only the guilty will be punished.[9] My assumption is that this need is no more necessary than a belief in creationism or in the salutary effect of the rain dance!

1.5 Good, Old Retribution

Many respectable politicians and criminal law experts believe that there must be a significant place for retribution in any criminal law system. And certainly the greatest part of the general population will share an attachment to 'an eye for an eye'. The justification might be couched in terms like 'fairness' or 'responsibility' or may represent a subliminal migration of religious thought into the secular affairs of crime and its prevention. Dostoyevsky's Crime and Punishment with its longing

9 Freedom and resentment.

for penance will resonate with many on the personal level. For many, peace of mind is only possible if their sins are neutralised by atonement.

It may be argued that a criminal law system conditioned primarily by forward-looking proportionality, that is, crime avoidance, fails to satisfy elements that are key to human existence. This is, however, not a real theme for possible relaxation of in dubio in reo, since such relaxation does not necessitate a belief that a criminal sanctions system must be motivated purely by utilitarian considerations. Retribution in its many primitive and sophisticated forms can still reign supreme, as long as it is accepted that retribution will sometimes hit the innocent in the endeavour to protect other innocent persons. A relaxation does not, in fact, mean less punishment. All things equal, it means more.

The more relevant objection could then be that *in dubio pro reo* breaches an equality principle, itself motivated by fairness. Like should be treated alike, and hence it would be wrong to punish somebody innocent, when otherwise only guilty persons would be treated in this fashion. That coin has another side as well, however. If all innocent individuals must be treated as innocent then also all criminals must be treated as such—and *in dubio pro reo* exactly hinders an approximation in this respect. *In dubio in reo* is inherently unfair from an equality perspective, but even more so because possible future victims are treated unequally when they do not get the protection of the law when they need it, although so many other citizens are shielded by the law in their hour of need. Leaving an innocent potential victim to his or her destiny when crime most likely could have been avoided by incarcerating a likely repeat offender is hardly a model of equality or fairness!

1.6 In Dubio Pro Reo, a Human Right?

For many *in dubio pro reo* may appear to be a human right on par with the presumption of innocence. In fact, eminent lawyers have in some instances unreflectively conflated the two concepts and stated that they are intrinsically linked. This is demonstrably not so. It is perfectly possible to preserve the presumption of innocence and operate strict criminal liability schemes, for instance, and this is done in many jurisdictions for defined offences. In these cases facts must still be proven beyond reasonable doubt, but culpability is assumed based on the mere existence of certain facts. The normal *mens rea* requirements are relaxed and conviction is possible although the defendant may not be guilty beyond reasonable doubt in the normal sense of these words. Still, human rights courts have not struck down strict criminal liability as incompatible with the presumption of innocence.

Presumption of innocence itself is explicitly defined as a human right in both the UN Covenant on Civil and Political Rights and the European Human Rights Convention. But it is a human right to be respected until proven guilty ‘according to law’, not until proven guilty beyond reasonable doubt. Thus both strict liability and a more general relaxation of *in dubio pro reo* are allowable. It may be argued that 'proven guilty' implies at least that there is a preponderance of evidence that the defendant is the perpetrator, and that is not a problem, but the presumption of innocence does not dictate how much '*dubio*' is required in order to necessitate finding '*pro reo*'. The law has considerable freedom in this respect.

The true human rights perspective is, again, the contrasting of the human rights of a suspect against the human rights of possible future victims. The right to life, liberty and health is not always trumped by due process rights!

1.7 Risk-Balancing in Practice

It is tempting to address the alternative to *in dubio pro reo* as a straightforward utilitarian equation, where the benefit to the potential victim is traded-off against the detriment to an accused who is potentially innocent. If there is a 51 % likelihood that the accused is guilty and there is certainty of recidivism, then the accused should be incarcerated, because there is then only a 49 % likelihood of error, and that is outweighed by the 51 % likelihood of averting further crime. Yet it is evident that we are now already speaking of an equation involving two variables—the likelihood of guilt and the likelihood of recidivism. But even this is far too simplistic. Further variables are the severity of the crime involved and the related societal interest in its avoidance; the severity of the remedy necessary in order to avoid repeat offences; the disgrace factor; the feeling of freedom factor and the feeling of justice discussed extensively above.

Spitting in public places is not a serious crime, despite opinion to the contrary in Singapore, and there would be no sensible reason to make shortcuts in the presumption of innocence in order to avoid repeat offences. Moving up the severity scale, however, the reasons for making shortcuts in *in dubio pro reo* become more and more compelling. Where there is a high probability of repeat murder, there is good reason to move close to the equation involving a 51 % likelihood, although it must be noted that the severity of the remedy plays a key role in this trade-off. If the only remedy for the possibly innocently accused would be the death penalty then, again, there is reason to move farther away from the 51 %. On the other hand, if the remedy would only be incarceration for two weeks, because the risk of recidivism was time limited, there might be good reason to move well below the 51 % likelihood. The most repugnant part of current *in dubio pro reo* thinking is that it makes absolutely no allowance for balancing the severity of possible repeat crime against the possible lightness of the avoidance remedy. If a murder could be avoided by locking up all the inhabitants of a village for 2 h, how could it possibly be justified not to do so? The practical lawyer will explain to you that there may be ways of producing the desired effect other than loosening up *in dubio pro reo*, such as use of policing or emergency powers, but that does not alter the fact that *in dubio pro reo* deliberately closes its eyes to the possibility of avoiding serious crime by means of a relatively light remedy at the expense of somebody who might, in all likelihood, be innocent. And, in most cases, the benefits of such a trade-off will not be realized through judicious use of policing or emergency powers, because the issue will not be identified at all, due to the mental shutters put on us by *in dubio pro reo*.

In fact, the only real concession criminal law has made to probability is in relation to preventive detention.[10] Preventive detention is often allowed in cases of serious crime, if the accused[11] is highly likely to have committed the crime and if there is a reasonably high degree of likelihood of repeat. The rationale for allowing preventive detention is that it is a provisional measure, one which does not conceptually prejudge the guilt of the accused, even if, as a safeguard for the accused, he must be the very likely perpetrator. Amazingly, even in these circumstances, Dworkin rejects the idea that preventive detention is ethically justified, and applies, in an even more inhuman fashion, the illogical reasoning of the German Constitutional Court already discarded above. Such aberrations aside, the example of preventive detention both discourages and encourages. It discourages because it stops where it stops, at the end of trial, for no coherent reason. Allegedly, it stops there because preventive detention should remain a provisional measure through which no permanent "damage" is done. In a transitional world, a distinction between permanent and transient damage is already conceptually flawed, and it is mind-boggling that one day you can be locked up as a probably guilty recidivist and the next day you can walk because there was reasonable doubt about your culpability, even though the risk you constitute remains the same. However, even if one looks instead at the severity of the damage done by a provisional measure, then it is by no means always less than the damage that may be done by a "non-provisional" measure. The haunting description of the protagonist's descent into hell in Tom Wolfe's *The Bonfire of the Vanities* is the best possible illustration of this. It is true that many legal systems foresee financial compensation in the case that preventive detention is not ultimately followed by a conviction, but the restorative effect is limited, and compensation is normally also available to persons who can eventually show that they were wrongly convicted. The possibility of compensation is thus clearly not a distinguishing feature.

In any case, there is a further problem with the provisional nature of preventive detention in that an indictment already sets the course for the social deroute, even if no preventive detention is associated with the indictment. Think about Wall Street's "perp walks". The criminal law system unblinkingly accepts that "permanent" damage can be done to an individual through his indictment, even if an indictment

[10] The prohibition of "consorting with known criminals" is a small step in this direction, since it punishes the likelihood that consorting with known criminals will lead to actual crime. It is, however, a very small step only, because it normally operates merely as a probation condition.

[11] Preventive detention after trial, which is a mode of sanction in many jurisdictions, is not relevant for the discussion of relaxation of *in dubio pro reo*, even if it aims at preventing repeat offences because it presupposes that guilt has been established, respecting *in dubio pro reo*.

requires only a much more modest degree of likelihood of ultimate guilt. It does so, reasonably, because this is the only way to make the system work well, yet there is no denying that the individual involved, when innocent, pays a heavy price: one which is less heavy if the perpetrator is ultimately found, but heavy indeed if the indicted individual is acquitted just because of a lack of proof.

The encouraging element of preventive detention is that it is an actual instance of relaxation of *in dubio pro reo* and that it debunks the pseudo-humanistic arguments of the German Constitutional Court and the seriously misguided Professor Dworkin. This notwithstanding, it must be remembered that preventive detention is not the silver bullet which renders further relaxation of *in dubio pro reo* unnecessary. Preventive detention is supposed to be relatively short-term (though often sinned against), it operates only within a very narrow range of delicts compared to the scope of *in dubio pro reo* and, importantly, does not carry the "signalling effect", or the same potential for individual or general deterrent, as does an actual conviction. A sexual offender who has endured preventive detention will not be deterred in the same fashion as he would have had he been found guilty and served a prison sentence, and possible future offenders will see relief.

Some crimes have faceless victims and might therefore appear to be less suitable for relaxations of *in dubio pro reo*. The avoidance of crimes against society as a whole does not have the same immediacy as the avoidance of debilitating crimes against individuals. Yet, curiously, society has often been far more inclined to sacrifice individual liberties in order to avoid damage to "the State" than to avoid damage to individuals. The root of this is a wonderful dichotomy between two misguided theories, that of the supremacy of the rights of the State and of *in dubio pro reo*. When collective rights are represented by the fiction of "State", there is an unreflective recognition that the interests of the collective must take precedence over the rights of the individual. As the sum of individual interests is represented through the State, it follows with almost mathematical logic that the interests of one individual can be sacrificed in order to serve this sum of interests. Not wrong *per se*, but handled carelessly when the soldier can become cannon fodder at the whim of a dictator or a malevolent majority, fuelled by the popular belief that State interest outweighs individual suffering. The absurd inflation of the concept of State has been a terrible facilitator of carnage throughout the centuries. The point here, however, is that the State, in the shadowy world of espionage, for example, is ready to play by a rule book in which individual rights are greatly downplayed in the perceived interest of protecting the State. Yet, when it comes to crimes against the State, such as tax fraud, *in dubio pro reo* is reinstated in all its glory, in spite of the fact that tax fraud constitutes a severe problem and although evidence is often so complex that *in dubio pro reo* has golden days. Loosening up the strictness of *in dubio pro reo* in cases of tax fraud could have very salutary effects on the avoidance of individual recidivism. But it could bring even bigger benefits in terms of general deterrence.

"Societal interest" is thus a variable which gains weight because convicting somebody who appears guilty, but might be innocent, sends a powerful message to other potential perpetrators that the likelihood of their being caught is greatly increased because *in dubio in reo* no longer provides such handy cover. Avoiding another murder is essentially a question of deterrence in a bilateral relationship, even if there is a secondary benefit of general deterrence, whereas it is the other way round when fighting tax fraud. A mature concept of *in dubio pro reo* would have to carefully weigh the benefits and relative weight of deterrence in both its forms.

The disgrace factor is, to some extent, dependent on the severity of the avoidance remedy, but it is also a factor that may be highly subjective. To a military man, honour will typically have a different value than to a con man. And it is generally assumed that honour in Japanese culture carries such a high value that much hardship will be endured in order to avoid disgrace. A loss of honour has very often led to hara-kiri in the past.

If one accepts the premise that all human action is dictated by self-interest, as many evolutionists do, it might appear entirely inconsistent that somebody can be ready to abandon his self because he has to give up honour. Yet there are evolutionary reasons why this can happen. All upbringing and conditioning essentially involves a system of approval and disapproval. The young child will endlessly repeat a newly learned routine, regardless of whether it fits the context, merely because the original demonstration of the new ability was associated with great acclaim. The young child uses its best tool to reap ever more acclaim.

Originally, acclaim was no doubt associated with getting food from parents, so that the search for acclaim was a necessary survival strategy. In human relations that are no longer motivated merely by the quest for food in order to survive, acclaim accompanies the acquisition of new skills and, as skills are a key determinant for social position, acclaim signals social progress. Concepts such as honour, or the significance of acclaim, tend to hypostasize, as does a concept like "State". When robbed of honour, life will, rightly or wrongly, lose its meaning for some. Yet, for a legal system to individualize reactive patterns depending upon individual susceptibility is inherently problematic. Must a soldier, for whom honour is paramount, be asked for less penal sacrifice than the criminal with a long record of convictions, for whom honour might mean nothing? Hand in hand with this goes the question of the wider social consequences of disgrace. Here, too, there is a wide variation in impact. A Prime Minister who is convicted of battery obviously suffers more severe social fallout than a soldier with no family, who is convicted of the same crime. Disgrace also involves secondary suffering, in the sense that the family and friends of a disgraced person in some way or other share in the disgrace. Young children will suffer more than adult family members, friends normally less than family. Can all these variables be taken account of in a mature concept of *in dubio pro reo*? Theoretically they should, but in reality there is no black and white answer. Social responses are often a conglomerate of individual considerations without any one consideration holding absolute sway. One consideration must be the wider social circumstances, but the countervailing element is obviously considerations of equality. The important point is, however, that the penal system is already attuned to these differentiations in general. The new element is that the disgrace might be incurred with a higher probability of innocence, which perhaps should lead to increased weight being given to the social fallout element.

In a holistic approach to damage avoidance, it is also logical, however, to consider the possible social fallout of not avoiding the crime. As the potential victim is not known, this cannot be individualized, but it is worth repeating the commonplace that some crimes, such as rape, carry social stigma for the victim and that the value of avoiding this stigma might be an off-setting element when considering the social stigma for any innocently convicted person.

1.8 Intuition and Counter-Intuition

This chapter claims for itself the luxury of dealing with relaxations of *in dubio pro reo* only on the conceptual level.

In practice, legal strategies and tactics for such relaxations are dependent on so many imponderables and varying national legal characteristics that it would be senseless to plot legal avenues before achieving a general understanding of the lack of ethical or logical foundation for strict adherence to *in dubio pro reo*.

In fact, this chapter cannot conclusively state that *in dubio pro reo* should be relaxed, it can only state categorically that the current theoretical foundation for strict adherence to *in dubio pro reo* does not hold up. However, there are arguments for classical *in dubio pro reo* that are so counter-intuitive, even anarchic, that they could actually be right.

Any criminologist would presumably agree that certain undesirable behaviour would have to attract a certain degree of societal sanction. The proportionality question is again what type of behaviour and what sanction? History and anthropology show the incredible bandwidth involved on both sides of that equation. Yet the blackout in New York in 1977, which resulted in immediate looting and mayhem, also seems to show the thinness of the veneer of civilization and the need for a system of credible sanctions. However, it is equally possible to argue that this incident shows how effective the system of oppression normally is, and that this sort of civil breakdown would not have taken place in nations with more equitable systems or stronger social cohesion. If a society attains the Marxist communist ideal, it may be argued that laws and sanctions are no longer relevant. A relaxation of *in dubio pro reo* could, from this perspective, be argued to only augment oppressive systems that necessarily lead us farther and farther away from the desired optimization of cumulative happiness.

In a rather perverse fashion, it could then be concluded that *in dubio pro reo* should only be relaxed in "just societies". Because of the regrettable lack of a commonly acknowledged deity willing to pronounce upon what is just and what is not, this is not a viable proposition. Yet the more palatable variation on this theme might be that relaxations of *in dubio pro reo* should not be contemplated in societies that are by definition unjust, that is, dictatorships.

It would be entirely respectable to argue that dictatorships should be deprived of a societal enforcement system, and consequently also of relaxations of *in dubio pro reo*. As it might be somewhat difficult to convince the dictator of this, the argument could be re-jigged to say that democracies should not even discus relaxations of *in dubio pro reo* because that might give dictators good ideas. The sad news is that dictators obviously had these ideas themselves long ago and, indeed, many have perfected the art of disregarding the link between guilt and punishment.

In a nice inversion of logic, it can then be said that democracies have put themselves at a competitive disadvantage to dictatorships, because the "juster society" is less capable of enforcing its norms than the unjust dictatorships. Anybody who lived in divided Germany in the 1970s and 1980s can bear witness to the inability of democracy to stem the tide of terrorism and the iron ability of dictatorship to enforce its norms. Not a desirable situation and, in the final analysis, certainly an argument against strict adherence to *in dubio pro reo*!

An argument with far more punch is the one that says that since prisons are schools of crime, and often themselves the venues for hideous crimes, then as few people as possible should be put through the experience. *In dubio pro reo* should become even stricter and the catalogue of crimes much shorter, while punishment, when meted out, should perhaps be even crueller in order to serve the interest of general deterrence in an otherwise "crime-light" society.

However, this argument is only really sound if one could believe that society has reached a level of civilization not dissimilar to the communist ideal, where there can be reliance on the inherent good of Man and reliance on societal structures not to distort the inherently good Man. If we had reached this state we would not, however, have such dreadful prisons, and the argument is thus circular.

Hence it seems that the path towards a truly harmonious society and a higher degree of cumulative happiness, requires prisons that educate towards the good and, hand in hand with this, a more balanced and effective enforcement of norms. A relaxation of *in dubio pro reo* could play a key role in the search for such a sublimation of justice!

Chapter 2
When a Crime is not a Crime

Abstract Necessity would appear to be an unambiguous concept. Yet in criminal law, where it serves as a justification for otherwise criminal acts if they bring high societal benefit, necessity only rarely brings acquittal. Historically there might be a good justification for this, but in evolved societies it would appear that necessity could be given a broader ambit, and thus enable a greater harvesting of societal benefits. The chapter argues that an expanded and well-balanced application of the necessity concept could bring not only more individual justice, but also be a catalyst of societal action to remedy systemic imperfections. The concern that wider application of the necessity defence would lead to anarchy is countered by the argument that post factum judicial control would be the ever-present corrective to over-enthusiastic resort to crime in the face of imagined injustice.

Keywords Necessity • Justification • Exculpation • Legal defence • Anarchy • Sanctity of property • Self-responsibility • Beyond good and evil • Proportionality • Compensation • *Nullum crime sine lege*

Positivism is a bulwark against anarchy. Every time positivism is sacrificed on the altar of naturalism the price is a degree of anarchy, as so tragically illustrated on the international scene a few years ago when a superpower opted for its perception of justice against clear, positive norms of international law.

Naturalism is thus not a viable option for maintaining societal order. Naturalism is the fuel of revolution. This notwithstanding, a question exists whether the principle of proportionality offers a hitherto under-appreciated dimension of positivism, allowing for predictable justice even when otherwise correctly promulgated norms would lead to demonstrable injustice. A permutation of sorts of naturalism.

The analytical starting point is the theory of self-defence, which is a well-tuned example of proportionality. Self-defence operates on the principle that an imminent illegal attack can be repelled by an equally illegal act, as long as the latter is not clearly disproportional to the original attack.

The pure example of proportionality in this respect is, however, the legal concept of necessity. Necessity is accepted as exculpation or justification for an illegal

P. Hulsroj, *The Principle of Proportionality*, SpringerBriefs in Law,
DOI: 10.1007/978-94-007-5775-2_2, © The Author(s) 2013

act undertaken in order to avert loss of a good of higher value than the one sacrificed by the illegal act. Necessity requires an imminent threat and an absence of other, better options to avert the loss.

On the face of it necessity is thus a most powerful tool to implement proportionality in value preservation across all societal domains. The values protected could be both tangible and intangible, could be goods, persons, intellectual property—even honour is alluded to in a related German statute. The illegal acts seeking to avert the damage could equally be of all kinds, could be the sacrifice of material or immaterial goods; or the causing of personal injury or death. The principle could even be a justification of torture.

Not surprisingly, legal systems around the world have not embraced the principle in this all-encompassing fashion, although it would be a strong remedy to the inevitable imperfections of the normative system. In desperate circumstances, the pure principle would possibly make it legal to rob a bank in order to buy medical treatment for a relative who would otherwise die.

The reason that legal systems have been more than reluctant to give necessity its full due is, of course, that the societal endeavour so far has been to get the inherently anarchic Man to follow the rules. Every let-out, self-defence, insanity, has been seen as a necessary evil. Individual judgment of whether a crime would be proportionally justified would further undercut the eminently positivistic alter ego of *nullum crime sine lege*, namely that law and law alone determines crime and punishment. As mentioned, this positivistic credo has already been somewhat undermined by the exculpation sanctioned by self-defence and, more problematically because of its entirely subjective nature, by the insanity defence. Yet, in terms of subjectivity the acceptance of the proportionality of crime in its pure form as invited by the necessity concept obviously introduces an exponential degree of complexity.

Common law and complexity go hand in hand, and lawyers from common law jurisdictions should thus be less aghast than civil law lawyers when considering the proportionality of crime. Common law lawyers might point out that where common law principles still permeate non-criminal law the province of common law in the criminal domain is waning, since most offences now are defined in statutes inter alia in order to decrease indeterminism. This distinction is, in itself, a questionable proposition since the indeterminism of common law in civil affairs might cause as much damage as in criminal law. Surely, many businessmen would prefer to go to jail innocent than to lose their businesses because of common law indeterminism in civil cases. But this is not really the point. The point is that the proportionality of crime introduces uncertainty about whether somebody undoubtedly guilty of a crime will actually be condemned. It does not alter *nullum crime sine lege*, and hence does not increase the risk of being criminally condemned. The uncertainty introduced is an uncertainty about whether society will punish the sacrifice of a good, even if the sacrifice leads to an overall societal gain.

From this point of view, it is easy to conclude that the proportionalisation of crime would lead to an even greater degree of anarchy than natural law. Law-abiding citizens may see themselves as robbed of the protection that criminal law normally affords to both person and property. Society may descend into a primitive state of "everybody for himself" because arbitrariness rules. Arbitrariness only rules, however, if we believe that it is an inherent feature of the proportionality of crime that every actor is the ultimate judge of the legality of his actions. Evidently this is not necessarily so. Courts would, of course, remain the arbiter of legality, and the individual would still have to predict the reaction of the courts when pondering the legality of his or her action. In this there is no difference between the situation in relation to self-defence, or to common law at large. The issue is whether we want a more bespoke system of justice, informed by the principle of proportionality. The price we would pay for a bespoke system is clearly a higher degree of uncertainty; the benefit we would gain is not only better justice, but also a corrective system that would allow blatant injustices to be identified, corrected and ultimately systemically addressed. If proportionality of crime would have been applied in the US, many criminal acts would have taken place in order to overcome the obvious injustice of the lack of comprehensive health care. The ultimate result would have been that the US in this field would have found a path to decency before the ascent of President Obama.

The degree of uncertainty to be paid for greater justice is, in fact, directly correlated to the degree of bespoke justice desired. If it is required that the benefit to be reaped far outweighs the crime, then the degree of uncertainty introduced is small; but if it is required only that the "cost" of the crime should be clearly less than the benefit, then the degree of uncertainty will be much higher.

The recognised principle of extenuating circumstances targets the same topology of reactions as proportionality of crime, but does so ineffectively and incompletely. Where proportionality of crime, and its sister principle self-defence, legitimate an avoidance action, extenuating circumstances signal societal disapproval—the signal being "Don't do it"! This might be sensible if society indeed wants to have the most minimalist avoidance system, with the resultant maximum of certainty and predictability. However, if society wants more bespoke justice, then the signal cannot be that you should not do something even if it is in the interest of cumulative happiness maximization, but if you do it nevertheless we might forgive you. If it is to work, bespoke justice requires a clear signal, and that signal must be "Do it if the benefit outweighs the societal cost to some established degree"!

2.1 Lord Denning and the Current Limits on the Necessity Defence

The famous English Master of the Rolls, Lord Denning, had a knack for putting things very succinctly even when it demonstrated how wrong he was. This ability he deployed well in a 1971 case, Buckoke v. Greater London Council, where in an *obiter dictum* he wrote:

> A driver of a fire engine with ladders approaches the traffic lights. He sees 200 yards down the road a blazing house with a man at an upstairs window in extreme peril. The road is clear in all directions. At that moment the lights turn red. Is the driver to wait for 60 seconds

> or more for the lights to turn green? If the driver waits for that time the man's life will be lost.... The circumstances go to mitigation and do not take away his guilt.

The reason a clever judge like Lord Denning can go so wrong is, of course, the fear of anarchy, if one starts to weaken the normativity of criminal offences. So, even if Lord Denning also stated that the driver should be commended, the overriding concern of Lord Denning was systemic integrity, and hence the conclusion that the driver was guilty. Yet, Lord Denning makes it too easy for himself, because he assumes that the driver would still do the right thing. But what if he did not? What if the driver waited for green and let the imperilled man die? In Lord Denning's logic he had the perfect defence: I acted in accordance with the law. By any normal logic the driver would have to be indicted for manslaughter, at least—and that is by no means by virtue of an extreme interpretation of the proportionality of crime principle.

What really disturbed Lord Denning he showed even clearer in another 1971 case, Southwark London Borough Council v. Williams, where the question was whether necessity made squatting legal. Lord Denning stated:

> If homelessness were once admitted as a defence to trespass, no one's house could be safe. Necessity would open a door no man could shut. It would not only be those in extreme need who would enter. There would be others who would imagine they were in need or would invent a need, so as to gain entry. The plea would be an excuse for all sorts of wrongdoing. So the courts must refuse to admit the plea of necessity to the hungry and the homeless: and trust that their distress will be relieved by the charitable and good.

Of course, exactly this sort of reasoning could have prevented self-defence as exculpatory, as well, but did not because of the a posteriori judicial control.

Still, one can see where Lord Denning and many other judges are coming from when they hold that:

> If the defence of necessity is to form a valid and consistent part of our criminal law it must, as has been universally recognised, be strictly controlled and scrupulously limited to situations that correspond to its underlying rationale.[1]

A society striving for compliance will not let illegality be accepted easily.

The upshot is that necessity as a defence is highly constrained. Breaking the window and entering a property in order to put out a fire is OK, driving under the influence in order to escape from a kidnap is OK, and the deeply tragic choice to let one Siamese twin live, when both cannot, is accepted. This is the kind of envelope within which the defence of necessity is currently operating, so, indeed, its application is scrupulously limited.

Still, as societies develop, what might have once been right and appropriate might not be ideal for the future—and societies must at least ask themselves whether their evolution would not allow more responsibility to be allocated to citizens and courts in terms of protecting higher goods even at the cost of permitting otherwise illegal acts in the pursuit of this objective.

---

[1] Perka v The Queen (1984) 2 SCR 232, Courts of Canada.

2.2 The Provenance of Crime as an Absolute

Early society was full of ambiguity in terms of crime. Councils of elders would hear complaints and provide radically bespoke justice. The penal "code" was the perception of justice as crystallized through the elders. Civilisation took a great step forward when the arbitrariness of this system was replaced by *nullum crime sine lege*. No longer would the legality of actions have to be gauged against the societal mood, but societal sanctions could be predicted by measuring them against positive norms.

As mentioned, there could be a fear that proportionality of crime would be a throw-back to these earlier, non-positivist days. This fear overlooks, however, that one part of the problem of that time was that crimes were defined "on-the-go". In contradistinction, proportionality of crime would not introduce uncertainty regarding *nullum crime sine lege*, it would only introduce uncertainty as to whether a crime has been committed, even *cum lege*. The principle is exculpatory. Furthermore, proportionality is not arbitrary. Proportionality requires good judgment, but it is not an empty norm without guidance, and the fact that good judgment is required for the operation of the proportionality principle does not set it apart from many other principles of criminal law, notably *in dubio pro reo* and the concept of negligence.

One of the reasons why proportionality of crime appears repugnant is that it collides with our intuitive understanding of equality. We believe that individual action and societal sanction must be balanced—that the same action must give rise to the same sanction. Insanity, for example, removes such equality, and hence the consequent exculpation does not threaten our view of equality as being mechanistic and eminently positivistic. Self-defence, again, does not threaten our perception of equality because the original illegal attack cancels out the illegality of the response. Only *necessity* seems to question our notion of the same action having to give rise to the same societal reaction.

Lord Denning was concerned with the risk of anarchy, but as the Southwark London Borough Council case shows, also with the sanctity of property. Where are we going to be if you were allowed to find shelter in my derelict building? Of course, expropriation operates on value proportionality, but then expropriation is controlled by the courts or some other official authority prior to the sacrifice of the demanded good. A priori control is the comfort normally offered to the possessed.

2.3 Parasitic Paternalism

There is an inherent comfort in knowing one's place. The insecure will flock to fatalism in order to remove the burden of self-responsibility. Absolutism was attractive because a cruel father figure would remove the cross of choice. Democracy has lightened the weight of this cross by making self-responsibility a shared responsibility. Schubert's rendition of Psalm 23, *The Lord is my Shepherd* stirs, on many levels, the wonderful feeling of being protected, even against our own folly.

Yet, in much religious thought there is not only the idea of the Lord's protection, but also the highly disconcerting threat of damnation unless you exercise your free will in the "right" way. Existentialism puts us at the eternal crossroads of choice, telling us that the individual must plot his own course. And modern society has so much choice and so much mutually exclusive advice that everyone can become his own subculture.

The cross-currents of submission and empowerment are the backdrop against which the concept of proportionality of crime must be judged. This is particularly so because, in a sense, proportionality of crime not only makes it legal to break the law, but also makes it a moral *obligation* to do so in certain circumstances, like that of Lord Denning's fire engine driver. Societies that have spent centuries moulding inherently anarchistic Man into a social animal will inevitably have difficulties with any proposition that loosens central control, especially because so much unintended loss of central control has been experienced as a result of the social experimentation that began in the 1960s. Drive-by shootings are a tragic consequence of "make love, not war". The anti-establishment movement of the 1960 and 1970s revolted against the parasitic paternalism of rigid hierarchical structures—and rightly so—yet replaced these structures with a culture largely premised on irresponsibility rather than self-responsibility. Sadly, it can be argued that the anti-establishment movement tried to move towards the communist ideal state of affairs long before the individual was ready for it, and long before the individual, in Marxist orthodoxy, had been returned to his original state of being inherently good. Ironically, Marxist and conservative thought is not so different in premising societal advancement upon rigid hierarchical structures, and the unfortunate legacy of not moving towards self-responsibility in a structured fashion is that a benevolent society has lost some of its ability to implement commonly agreed measures for individual betterment.

The starting point of societal engineering must, however, be the conditions prevailing at a given time. In terms of the proportionality of crime, the question is whether, in a societal state of irresponsibility, an expansion of this individualistic principle would lead to more self-responsibility or whether, it would become a shortcut to even more irresponsibility. Although, the proportionality of crime is, of course, but a small piece of the societal puzzle, the question is similar to the one which the anti-establishment movement neglected to ask itself: can individuals generally shoulder the burden of self-responsibility?

The answer might depend on an assessment of the state of justice. If the assumption is that bespoke justice is much needed in order to remedy systemic imbalances, the answer might be that the individual *must* shoulder the burden of self-responsibility, and that the societal gain from the exercise of self-responsibility must not necessarily wildly outweigh the societal price associated with allowing an otherwise illegal act. But then "must" is different from "can", and the question was whether the individual *can* shoulder the burden. The answer might then be one straight out of the proportionality book, namely that many might not be able to shoulder the burden, but that this is a price society must pay in order to realize the much more important benefit of bespoke and corrective justice. A very uncomfortable conclusion indeed! The answer should probably be the opposite, however; namely, that if a society is in dire need of systemic improvement in order to cater for proper justice, then the remedy is not for everybody to reach for their own gun in order to provide for individual justice. If the problem is despotism, the collective means of revolution might be the right medicine, and if the problem is a lack of proper institutions, then obviously the remedy is not to erode the nascent institutions by asking for a much higher degree of sophistication through the medium of proportionality of crime. Do not give someone a trawler if he cannot yet use a fishing rod!

In fact, proportionality of crime presupposes a society already fine-tuned in terms of justice. Only then will the exercise of this principle be an exception, and only then is it responsible policy vis-à-vis individuals who, due to social conditioning, should abhor breaking the law even when it is done for the noblest of reasons! The foundation of the human being as a social animal is, as mentioned, fragile. Still, it is clearly also correct to note that, in many other respects, society now demands much more mature and personal decision-making, even by society's weakest. The Clintonian welfare model of providing for the stricken only if they themselves are ready to contribute to society, places existential decisions in the hands of every individual, irrespective of capability. New sexual mores, and attendant deadly diseases, mean that individuals, even at an early age, might have to grapple with sexual identity and learn to balance pleasure against serious risk. Religious doctrine has become amazingly optional. With such a state of affairs, it is presumably not too much to ask that individuals, in rather rare cases, might have to resist prima facie societal instruction in order to realize a higher goal of justice!

Anarchy is not going to be the consequence, even if it is true that proportionality of crime represents a further small step towards the anarchical ideal of a society that operates mostly on individualized social contracts. But then, of course, the anarchical dream is nothing but idealized humanism or, if you wish, completely bespoke justice. The premise, a complete realization of the inherently good in Man, has been far from realized by any societal model, but proportionality of crime allows for finer justice, and for a slightly more discerning, slightly more mature and caring human being. Gradualism as a means of human betterment is not a bad idea!

2.4 Typology

Self-interest has an unfortunate tendency to mess up concepts that are otherwise good. The Marxist road to a self-interest-free society leads into the wilderness, because tyranny of the proletariat is no probative step to rein in self-interest.

Conceptually, proportionality of crime would, no doubt, raise far fewer hackles if only disinterested parties could be players, and self-interest could thus be eliminated. A situation in which an individual commits a crime in order to assist a third party, with the result that a net societal gain is realized, is much easier to accept than a situation in which an individual commits a crime for his own benefit, even if a net societal gain is equally the result.

Yet, it is neither appropriate nor possible to draw a line of legality between the two situations, and hence to declare as legal only the situation involving disinterested parties. It is not possible to draw a line because it would be an invitation to circumvention: getting your cousin to hold the gun, rather than holding it yourself! It is not appropriate to draw a line, because often the friendless will be the one most in need.

It might be advisable, however, to establish a different threshold of net societal gain in the two situations. The person who acts out of self-interest should perhaps be required to show that the crime he committed brought a more obvious net societal benefit than the person who tried to help somebody else. In a sense, this would be an inversion of the situation prevailing with self-defence. The doctrine of self-defence dictates that the force used to repel the illegal attack shall not be clearly disproportionate to the threat, but it is accepted that when one protects oneself one might go a bit overboard. The reason why the doctrine of self-defence is more indulgent of the interests of the attacked person is, of course, that he is subjected to an illegal attack, and hence it is found just that the attacker might suffer a somewhat disproportionate loss, merely because "he asked for it". In proportionality of crime, the victim of the loss off-setting crime is entirely innocent, and a difference in the threshold of net societal gain between self-interested and disinterested actors might be justified by the societal interest in avoiding that self-interest gets the better of the ideal.

However, it is crucial to note that the concern that self-interest might mess up an otherwise good concept has not stopped those defining legal doctrine from accepting self-defence as exculpatory. The person defending himself against an illegal attack is himself under the threat of criminal sanction, if the force used to repel the attack significantly exceeds the reasonability standard. Conceptually, there is no difference between this penal threat and the penal threat that would be associated with crimes committed by self-interested parties, if the crimes bring no clear net gain to society.

A central feature of many implementations of necessity, which by definition involves only innocent parties, is that the beneficiary of the exercise has to compensate the possible loss to those whose goods have been sacrificed. Compensation might not always be feasible in practice, however. This notwithstanding, a poor person must also be able to invoke proportionality of crime. If a wealthy person can break someone's arm in order to save his own life, and then be obliged to pay monetary compensation for the injury and pain suffered by the victim, then so can a poor person, even if he cannot pay the compensation. Here, too, the decisive element is whether there is a net societal gain. In this example, the poor person may benefit at the expense of the victim, yet the only thing that ultimately matters is the net societal gain. Both injurer and victim are innocent at the outset, and whether compensation can be paid is only a question of the eventual luck or misfortune of the victim. For society, the net gain is there, irrespective of the possibility of compensation, and this is true even when the trade-off is ultimately only a financial one.

When a concert pianist who is excusably late for a concert steals a bike in order to still make it, the monetary value of the bike and the sacrifice of societal value in allowing a theft are potentially dwarfed by the value of having the concert take place. In this situation proportionality of crime would exculpate as long as the concert pianist gave back the bike and paid for the bus ticket of the stranded bike owner. On the other hand, when a millionaire steals a Ferrari in order not to be late for a golf game, proportionality of crime does not exculpate, even if the millionaire pays generous compensation, simply because no net societal gain has been achieved.

Proportionality of crime is wonderfully democratic!

2.5 Beyond Good and Evil

The norm-relativity of Nietzsche might be said to chime well with proportionality of crime. Proportionality of crime might be thought to introduce exactly the kind of normative fluidity that is the central theme of *Beyond Good and Evil*. Outside of metaphysics it is, however, a fundamental mistake to believe that relativity contrasts the absolute. Relativity primarily concerns itself with the relationship between absolutes, and introduces predictive fluidity when one analyzes how two absolutes interact. Relativity does not bring lawlessness, neither in physics nor in law. Gravity and mass may interact, but each nevertheless has inherent properties, as illustrated by the fact that a given mass, when exposed to a given degree of gravity will always "weigh" the same. Relativity is only meaningful if the interacting elements have some inherent properties and, even in quantum mechanics, the problem is not an absence of inherent properties, but the mystery of (the absence of) the relativity.

Proportionality of crime has everything to do with rule-bound relativity and nothing to do with normative fluidity. Proportionality of crime puts a criminal norm, with inherent features, into a relationship with a protectable good, also with its own inherent features. As a result, the validity of the inherent features of the criminal norm is confirmed. To the extent that the exercise of a norm invigorates it, proportionality of crime also does exactly that. And to the extent that the degree of justice in a system determines its strength, proportionality of crime can be a positive contributor. But, as with strong medicine, it should only be given to a strong patient!

"Render unto Caesar the things which are Caesar's, and unto God the things that are God's" was the way of Jesus to avoid confronting the tension between morals and law, which in the centuries before and after has been a crucible for endless bloodshed. Natural law was a way of seeking to fuse morals and law, but is, in the final analysis, purely a pretext for the imposition of subjective views. Yet, as counterintuitive as it may sound, in its own limited domain proportionality of crime aligns moral exigencies with law, without succumbing to pure naturalism.

Chapter 3
Love and Proportionality

Abstract Love is disproportion! Love of tribe leads to love of country, and love of country leads to sovereignty as an inalienable good. However, sovereignty leads to dismemberment of the international community, and ultimately to a lack of empathy for the stricken of other sovereignties. This chapter posits that concepts like *jus cogens* and *erga omnes*, correctly understood, remove the comfort of being protected from cries for help by the walls of sovereignty, and that *erga omnes* obligations are not only obligations on all countries but also on all constituent elements of countries: institutions, corporations and, not least, each individual. When someone dies from hunger it is the failing of all of us! Those fundamental human rights which individuals can fulfil are incumbent on us all and should be enforceable against us all—even legally. The nearest neighbour who could help should ultimately be responsible, but everybody should be obliged to provide relief if able to do so, even if the ultimate bill might have to be covered by the nearest neighbour. That is love's dictate!

Keywords *Erga omnes* • Jus cogens • Sovereignty • Marginal utility • Human rights covenants • Universal declaration of human rights • Proportionality • Dualism • Litigation • Responsibility to protect • Tribe

Love is disproportion (as is hate)! Those of us who love ourselves look in the mirror with rose-tinted glasses, or rather use the mirrors of amusement parks which broaden our shoulders and narrow our hips. Those of us who love others relish their virtues and downplay their vices. Emotions, and none more than love, categorize virtue and vice in proportion to individual preference, not in proportion to the optimization of societal happiness. So love can be said to be an ultimate expression of individual perceptions of proportionality, but also an expression of distortion from a societal perspective.

What to do then if one is striving for dispassionate proportionality for the purpose of fashioning a society of optimized collective happiness? Must we reject emotion and seek to rein in love in order to optimize the common wealth of happiness? Must we become stoics in order to create an ethical society or allow Buddhist release from desire to find us in order to best fulfil the desires of the majority?

P. Hulsroj, *The Principle of Proportionality*, SpringerBriefs in Law,
DOI: 10.1007/978-94-007-5775-2_3, © The Author(s) 2013

When asked in this way, the question may seem absurd and the negative answer obvious. But consider it from the perspective of one of the most prominent questions in utilitarian theory: William Godwin's question on whether a son should save his mother or the Archbishop of Cambrai, when only able to save one of them from a burning house.[1] Emotion would dictate the mother, reason the Archbishop.

Luckily, we might not need to choose between love and reason here, because our theme is only to what extent an allowance must be made for love in our proportionality equations and in our societal design. And it would indeed be ridiculous if, in the pursuit of the highest degree of common happiness, we would seek to eliminate love and the striving for love, when love is the strongest vehicle for individual and collective happiness.

What we must do is understand love's domain and its future proper empire!

3.1 Does Love Exist?: And Does It Matter?

You recognize love when you meet it. Coming-of-age books gently explain symptoms and codes of conduct. Grown-up literature has, as a perennial topic, the complexities of finding and managing love. Yet good science does not like truths that are accepted too readily, and evolutionary theory has thus put a question mark against the very idea of love. Love might be only a purpose-built mirage feeding self-serving aims. All of love might turn on the existential need to pass-on genes. Not only might love of offspring be so motivated, but a woman's love of red is also conditioned by evolutionary needs, because, as collectors of food, her ancestors looked for ripe fruit, which tends to be reddish. The survival of the genes is thus served! Interesting studies in Finland have shown an increased mortality rate for grandmothers at the time when their grandchildren gain substantial personal independence; the assumption being that some grandmothers die when they no longer have a childcare function vis-à-vis the grandchildren. So love serves gene survival, even one generation removed. All this is interesting, but fortunately does not ultimately replace the phenomenon of love that we, perhaps by evolutionary processes, have internalized as our most important actual feeling. It can be argued that love as a true feeling can exist only if we do not credit too fully whatever evolutionary mechanism might, or might not, be involved. Pity the scientist who, by explaining, eliminates the object of his science.

For the purposes of our investigation, the importance of looking beneath the surface of the phenomenon of love is that it may render important information on why society is constructed the way it is—and might even show a path towards further improvement.

---

[1] Enquiry concerning political justice.

3.2 Love as a Force for Good

If love reigned supreme, there would be no taxes, because no taxes would be needed. Man would take care of his fellow man without the need for state intervention. Along these lines, Peter Singer has advanced the idea of marginal utility, by suggesting that the riches of the world should be distributed in such a fashion that each individual should only consume a good if this consumption would bring him greater utility than consumption of the same good by somebody else[2]; part of the communist ideal state achieved by strict adherence to utilitarian principles, in fact.

This is obviously a pipe dream—and one based on error—because the assumption is that you love those far away as much as those nearest to you. Love would become less emotional, more abstract and hence less motivating. Societal design should not aim at restraining the most powerful enabler of good, but should channel and reinforce emotion to achieve the highest general benefit and, at the same time and for the same reason, the highest individual emotional satisfaction.

The better way of looking at love's function is actually to assume the self-evident: that the strength of love is a function of emotional proximity and that it thus tends to diminish as it becomes more universal. The love of self and of kin is the inner circle, surrounded by circles of increasing abstraction and hence of watered-down emotion.

If one adopts this stance, there is a paradox to overcome. Why is a person ready to die for his country or for an abstract idea? Or, more fundamentally, is love well applied when a person is led to make this sort of self-sacrifice?

When people die for religion it is perhaps understandable, even from the perspective of self-love, because the reward is understood to be eternal salvation. The cost–benefit analysis shows a huge preponderance of benefit. Much speculation has gone into such calculations, as witnessed by the mass of literature on Pascal's Wager, which purports to show that it is logical to bet on eternal salvation, even if the sacrifice required is very high. This logic does not explain why people are ready to die for their country, however. A country can only reward the sacrifice by erecting a statue or by encouraging the wearing of poppies in November. That one's remains will be:

some corner of a foreign field
That is for ever England[3]

seems to be small consolation for the prospect of eternal extinction, no matter how deep the love of country.

Yet, the depth of love is presumably the answer to the puzzle. Thankfully, love of country is, in our day and age, less and less of an inducement to make the ultimate

---

[2] Famine, affluence, and morality, in Unsanctifying human life.

[3] Rupert Brooke, The soldier.

sacrifice, simply because the feeling has become less pronounced. With love, whether consciously or unconsciously, we seem to operate our own cost–benefit analyses, in which we make an assessment of whether the love felt in a particular situation is more or less abstract, and hence more or less directly felt, and we weigh against this the risk or cost involved in accommodating love. In this roundabout fashion, proportionality still reigns, even in matters of love, and our task becomes one of examining whether the allocation of the capital of love is rational, even though we acknowledge that in one sense love is not rational because it is an expression of subjective preference. The point is that despite the subjective preference involved, love can be allocated in a more or less effective manner. Sad though it may be to say, love can be commoditized and the pool of love can be managed and distributed more or less effectively, just like all other types of capital. All that has to be kept in mind is that the strength of love is a function of emotional proximity.

This is not evolutionary theory, but it is related to it, because evolutionary theory assumes a readiness to sacrifice that is directly proportionate to gene survival. The higher the proportion of genes that survive, the higher the readiness to sacrifice, be it the sacrifice of self or of other kin. Beyond reproductive age, therefore, the readiness to sacrifice the self should be high.

The thesis in our examination is, however, broader and more phenomenological in that it is assumed, as in evolutionary theory, that love can be commoditized, but unlike in evolutionary theory, it is assumed that the commoditization is not a mere reflection of the prospects of gene survival. What else enters into the commoditization equation does not matter here, because we stay rigidly phenomenological: what we see is what we believe!

There is another paradox that needs to be mentioned in relation to effective capital allocation, and that is that an unwillingness to sacrifice for love sometimes serves the purpose of love. In development economics, it is well known that huge income from natural resources generally gets in the way of development. Both in development economics and in finance in general, the principle of diminishing rates of return is commonplace. In the stock market, companies might buy back shares or pay extraordinary dividends because the company has reached a stage where it cannot sensibly deploy further capital. So riches are sometimes counterproductive. The same is true of love. The parent who mistakes indulgence for love does the child no good, even if, in a sense, the indulgence is an expression of misplaced or excessive love. A decreased willingness on the part of the parent to indulge the child will have disproportionally high returns. There is such a thing as too much of a good thing, which does not go to say that love cannot be felt as boundless.

In the broader societal scheme of things, an unwillingness to sacrifice in the name of love can also sometimes lead to great benefit.

Leaders and men of war have long been happy to make pure utilitarian calculations, even before Machiavelli elevated the pursuit of ends to an art, and they relied on the emotion and the sacrifice of their subjects to give effect to their belligerent calculations. The calculations were short or mid-term in nature, and scant attention was given to systemic effects. Machiavelli advocated relative advantage, without contemplating the wider issue of how the quest for immoral relative advantage leads to ruinous anarchy for all when it becomes conventional wisdom.

From the perspective of those who are the cannon fodder, the requested sacrifice might have made sense when material survival was at stake: better to die in combat while seeking to secure survival of self and kin, than for all to passively starve to death. And in fact the mercenary's logic has prevailed for most of human history, against the backdrop of pervasive poverty throughout the ages. With the progress of the industrial revolution, proportionality could no longer justify the risk of self-sacrifice, however. Instead, kings and generals almost paradoxically invoked the love of king and country to ask for sacrifice, although this made little sense in terms of cool-headed calculation—Machiavelli would have shaken his head in disbelief. Still, king and country turned out to be powerful motivators in their own right because they have roots in tribal thinking. The concept of tribe is possibly the greatest invention of "thinking beasts" because it makes cooperation possible, and because it also makes possible the pursuit of common survival against external dangers. The march of civilization was predicated on tribe. And the glue of tribe in its human form is love, not necessarily of each member of the tribe, but of the idea of the tribe to which one belongs. So, even after tribe had developed into something far more abstract, with far less tangible benefits for the individual member, that is, king and country, the long period of conditioning made it possible to appeal to love and therefore to demand sacrifice. The horrifying readiness to follow the near-term calculations of king and country onto the battlefield has made for the immense misery of war wrought during the 20th century; it continues today as illustrated by the horrifying ease with which the last war in Iraq was started.

Still, there is a competing reality, which is the decreasing readiness of the well-educated and well-fed to rally to the clarion call of the realm. This decreasing readiness is not necessarily due to cowardice or comfort, but due to an increasing, if perhaps self-serving, understanding of the longer-term effects of war. The starting point for this understanding can be found in three Biblical pieces of wisdom, which appear to be loaded with mutual tension. The first is the stern Old Testament prescription "An eye for an eye", the second is the New Testament's admonition "to turn the other cheek", and the last is the wonderful question: "Why do you look at the speck of dust in your brother's eye, with never a thought for the great plank in your own?". Proportionality informs all three statements. Yet, are they relevant for how we deal with war, or even with love? Is not war antithetical to "turning the other cheek" and love antithetical to "An eye for an eye"? And is love not all about seeing the speck of dust in your own eye, rather than the plank in the eye of the other?

If you want to be pedantic about it you could argue that "turning the other cheek" and "looking at the speck of dust" are mutually supportive statements and that "an eye for an eye" is the odd man out. And, of course, the Old Testament is generally not a testament to humanism, whereas the New Testament is a pinnacle. This notwithstanding, the Bible often works on many levels, with the Old Testament being a toolbox for self-assertiveness and pro-activity, while the New Testament centres on modesty, forgiveness and reactivity. What appear to be mutually exclusive prescriptions are more a catalogue of reactive patterns, all with potentially ethical uses, depending on the circumstances. Anybody who has embraced the human spirit of another individual for any length of time will acknowledge that a relationship may sometimes be better served by "an eye for an eye", sometimes by the turning of the other cheek, but is *always* better served by remembering how frighteningly easily we see the speck of dust in the eye of the other. The terribly difficult thing is to know when an eye for an eye is called for and when the other cheek. The lesson of the Bible is that because of the plank in the own eye one should normally err on the side of the other cheek.

Notwithstanding former President Bush's devotion to the Old Testament, over a long period of time, humanism has glacially moved us towards the pre-eminence of turning the other cheek. Many well-educated and well-fed have learned in their private and professional lives that there is a long-term benefit in tending towards the other cheek, because it reduces the risk of mutual destruction, and they will naturally transpose this realization to the wider political perspective as well. They will be reluctant to go to war and to risk death for their country, simply because they have learned that, in the long run, aggregated misery will be the result. You should only put your beef at risk if it does not make your long-term enjoyment of the beef unlikely. That is the chapter Machiavelli did not write.

It is true that when judiciously assessed, Hitler's abuse of Chamberlain demonstrates that there is a case for an "eye for an eye", yet the preceding Great War was an example of how well it would have served humankind to have turned a few more cheeks. Had this been the case, then the need for "an eye for an eye" 20 years later would have been avoided and Hitler could have been allowed to peacefully pursue his postcard-painting skills.

In an age of radical Islam, it is not easy to be a pacifist. It is easy to see the speck of dust in many eyes, but when seriously discussing proportionality one must start with a look at the plank in one's own. And the plank of the rich and predominantly secular world has all to do with love as a force for evil, absurd as it may sound.

3.3 Love as a Force for Evil

When presiding over an unjust world, one must be careful in condemning the unjust actions of the disenfranchised, lest the plank get the better of you.

Actions by the disenfranchised, which are disproportional in response to an alleged wrong, will appear to the perpetrator as a proportional reaction to his general state of despair. Those with privileges to defend must therefore address the state of despair, even if acting from their own narrow perspective of selfishness. The question is why, in view of proportionality, this has not been done as a matter of course.

Part of the answer to this is that we assume that love stops at the water's edge. Tribal instincts require that there is a physical "enemy" against which the tribe can compete. This is admittedly not a necessary ingredient for tribalism, but it is an element that has been deeply instilled in us over thousands of years of essentially tribal competition for survival. The greatest impediment to the creation of a truly global society is that there would be no tribe left to compete against. The absence of an external physical enemy makes it almost impossible to mould a global society, because the inevitable departures from received wisdom and the sacrifice of acquired privileges seem unjustified in the absence of a need to defend against some external pressure. If Martians invaded the earth, a global defence would be put together within the shortest period of time, and a global society would be the result.

Terrorism has tragically illustrated this point. Terrorism in its present-day form knows no boundaries, but seeks to exploit the boundaries maintained by its adversaries. If we look at the developments that have taken place over the last 10 years, we find that terrorism has acted as an external pressure on a community, which then started to look like a global tribe, albeit only in this narrow field. It is remarkable that a US Administration that had philosophically rejected multilateralism, then moved NATO to act as one in Afghanistan, created a coalition of the willing in Iraq, and showed a great will to tackle cross-boundary issues as long as it was justified by the fight against terrorism.

This willingness to act jointly is entirely in line with tribal instincts, because states unite to fight a physical enemy. Yet, in some situations, it is also wise to fight your enemy's enemy because it might make him your friend. From a tribal perspective, the problem with this is that the enemy of this particular enemy is poverty and lack of a future and, since the enemy is not physical, it is so much harder for the tribal being to understand the need to fight the terrible enemy of your enemy. Imagine that the Middle East was threatened by the Martian invasion. Can there be any doubt that we would rush to the rescue and that we would be ready to sacrifice enormous sums in order to repel the enemy, as was done in Afghanistan and Iraq? Love feeds off proximity, and the enemy—poverty and lack of a future—is hard to feel and visualize, when you are sitting comfortably, far, far away.

The concept of national sovereignty is the last bastion of tribal enemy thinking. National sovereignty is the most dangerous barrier standing between humankind and a truly global community. Ultra-liberals might argue that state competition is nothing more than Adam Smith scaled-up to the state level, and that competition between nations is good, just as competition between individuals is healthy. This is obviously a wild distortion. Competition between states has some benefits, because it becomes a competition between political ideals or between modes of government. This has value. But from the Adam Smith perspective there is very little value in economic competition between states, if state involvement is purely one of distorting the competition between individuals. The track record of states is, in fact, mainly that. It is not the optimization of global competition or welfare that is sought, but relative advantage along the lines of Machiavelli. The state seeks the best for its particular tribe, not for all tribes, let alone for all individuals.

Globalization is on its way to bringing all tribes closer together, yet it is a wonderful testimonial to traditional tribal thinking that dominant tribes have put much stronger adjudication mechanisms in place to protect their tribal investments than to protect peace, international justice and humanitarian obligations. The functional disparity between WTO arbitration and ICJ adjudication is both grotesque and, at the same time, a sign of hope. In proper proportionality it is, of course, unacceptable to value effective regulation of commerce more highly than the effective regulation of all other aspects of human intercourse. Nevertheless, hope is created by the increasing proximity signalled by WTO arbitration. The WTO is, in the final analysis, a small step towards abandoning the semi-religious adoration of sovereignty. Still, much bigger steps are needed, and needed quickly, because of the inhumanity and danger involved in Third World poverty and other global imbalances. For reform to take place, it is important that we understand why and where the concept of sovereignty has led us astray.

National sovereignty protects national cultural identity, in addition to being the ultimate tool for gaining relative advantage vis-à-vis other groups. The decolonisation process in the second half of the 20th century found the concept of sovereignty to be a most powerful ally in the fight against imperialism. And we have grown fond of thinking that the reward for de-colonisation was that national cultural identities were restored, and through this, that the dignity of the formerly oppressed was restored, as well.

What we forget was that through de-colonisation, the former colonial masters gained easy absolution, akin to the way in which a conglomerate divests itself of a troublesome subsidiary. The newly independent states were left to fend for themselves, with sovereignty being their tool for seeking relative advantage against, inter alia, the former colonial powers and other fully industrialized countries. Small wonder that most of them got left behind.

To this day, the accepted wisdom is that sovereignty must be respected at all costs. Article 2.5 of the UN Charter has codified this terrible, if politically correct, thought. The net result is that many populations in developing countries are left to be exploited by their own corrupt elites, without the need for well-meaning prosperous countries to conclude that they could or should do something effective about it. Mugabe's megalomaniac rape of his own country is an extreme, but not entirely unique symptom of the blessings of sovereignty for populations in the developing world.

This is not to say that the concept of sovereignty is entirely devoid of merit. It is right and proper that nations should be the first to assist their respective populations, and it is right and proper that tribes are allowed to protect their own cultures and define their own models of governance. This is within love's dictate. What is unacceptable is that nations are left to their own devices even when their models of governance are manifestly dysfunctional and corrupt, or when disaster strikes and the affected nations cannot cope alone. In those situations, sovereignty fatally distorts proportionality, and frustrates not just Peter Singer's marginal utility, but the marginal love that a tribe would otherwise have for another stricken tribe.

3.4 What Must, Should or Could be Done

One of the most extraordinary distortions brought about by the concept of sovereignty has, as its starting point, a perversion of the message of the Universal Declaration of Human Rights and the Covenants derived from the Universal Declaration.

The UN Charter saw the elimination of war as the key to human welfare, and not wrongly so. As war is based on the concept of military competition of sovereignties, the UN Charter is highly state-centric. The Universal Declaration and the subsequent Covenants on Civil and Political Rights and on Economic, Social and Cultural Rights took a welcome step beyond the focus on war by drawing attention to the multitude of ingredients in human welfare apart from being free from violent death as a result of war.

However, neither the Universal Declaration nor the Covenants are particularly state-centric in their proclamation of the rights accorded to each individual by virtue of being a human being in a society of human beings.

Yet, because we are used to thinking in terms of sovereignty, the astounding—and almost universal—interpretation of all three legal instruments has been that the rights declared for each individual are rights in respect of the tribe, the home or host state, not rights which can be invoked *erga omnes* or, more to the point, not obligations on the international community towards each of its individual members.

Although it is logical and right to assume that the responsibility for fulfilling human rights lies first and foremost with the home or host state, which is, in any case, the only entity capable of conferring the required civil and political rights in the current design of the international system, if we are serious about the inalienable nature of human rights, we must also recognize that the obligation to ensure the enjoyment of human rights by each individual rests with all entities in human society, from the microscopic level of other fellow beings to the meta level of the international community as such.

There is much to be said about how and whether such obligations can be called upon from a process perspective, but that does not detract from the imperative view that the legal obligation rests upon us all.

Imagine the situation in which you pass someone who is dying from starvation, but do not share your surplus of bread with him. Is that a moral infraction and perhaps even a legal one? Compare the situation with one where you see somebody drowning. You could have saved the person, but you did not. Most people would say that this would constitute a moral infraction, and in Denmark, as opposed to the United States, you would have committed a crime.

Now, in wealthy Denmark, if you had left someone to die from starvation when you could have avoided it, you would again have committed a crime as long as the starving person was encountered in Denmark, but not if the starving person was in Sudan and you were in Denmark.

This sort of dilemma has led Peter Singer to define his marginal utility principle: only consume a good if it provides you with more benefit than if the good were consumed by somebody else. However, most other people reject this notion and make sense of the dilemma by resorting to the good old exculpatory and tribal principle of sovereignty. Yet, even if one believes in the principles enunciated in the Universal Declaration and the two Covenants, Peter Singer's marginal utility principle is still not mandatory, and resorting to the principle of sovereignty is wrong.

The solution is once again love as a function of proximity.

On the moral as well as on the legal plane we assume that the question of obligation has a binary answer: either we have it or we don't. Peter Singer says that we have a moral obligation to follow the principle of marginal utility by virtue of being human beings who have responsibility for other human beings, and that the failure by other human beings to respect marginal utility does not excuse us. With this as the starting point, the obligation becomes both very abstract and, if applied to the legal side of the equation, dangerously misleading.

As discussed above, with abstraction goes a lack of emotional engagement, which in practice will lead to fracture with the possible moral norm; this is particularly true when the moral dictate would lead all followers to a life akin to that of Mother Teresa. It clearly does not help in the fight against poverty to set the moral crossbar so high that our love cannot clear it. But it is equally jarring with love's dictate to assume that we must help our tribal brother who is 500 m away, but not help the member of the neighbouring tribe who is drowning 500 m away on the other tribe's territory. This is why sovereignty is, in the main, morally irrelevant. Morality might allow that you save the member of your tribe before the member of another tribe, but not that you let the member of a neighbouring tribe die when, without any great sacrifice or risk, you could have saved him. The difference between this and the principle of marginal utility is that you are morally sanctioned to save the one you love the most first—the mother before the Bishop. And as love is a function of emotional proximity, you are thus also justified in saving members of neighbouring tribes before those of distant tribes. If one then flips this to deal with obligation instead of permission, one finds that the ever-widening circles of love, decreasing in strength as they move farther and farther away from their originator, would form an all-encompassing pattern of love when considering all originators, and this makes the obligation to assist members of distant tribes secondary to the obligation to assist the ones most loved, because those least loved by you would be those most loved by others.

When the love of others fails, our marginal love becomes invocable, but only for what is, and must remain, a secondary obligation both in the sense of becoming relevant only when others fail, but also in the sense of not having to be met with the same force or level of sacrifice as the primary obligation to assist the ones most loved. If sovereignty has a role to play in this equation then it is only as a unit allowing us to measure how close or far away one tribe is relative to another.

As is often the case with proportionality, the relativity equation consists of more than one relationship. In addition to proximity, the level of distress must also be factored-in. The human being dying from starvation in a distant land will have little sympathy for the idea that his salvation is a function of proximity: that his fellow man who is far away is not obliged to save him, even when this would amount to only a slight inconvenience, and that his excuse for this would be that another fellow man, one nearer at hand, should have saved him. Relativity that allows the stricken to bear the risk for the failure of a fellow man is unacceptable. It may then be argued that this returns us to the marginal utility proposed by Peter Singer, and the demand for every moral human being to live in saintly abstinence. Interestingly, law gives us the answer to this dilemma. In a general sense, it is assumed that an individual's moral obligations are independent of his legal obligations—indeed, that moral obligation generally exceeds legal obligation—and that moral obligation sometimes means that law must be broken. In this instance, however, law explains moral obligation and makes the moral obligation real and realistic. The key to resolving the tension between humanitarian dictate and human achievability is to understand the relationship between right and the process for enforcing right.

In the coding system of international law, *jus cogens* and *erga omnes* signify the highest normativity. *Jus cogens* means that the norm in question cannot ever be deviated from, either by treaty or other form of agreement. *Erga omnes* means that an obligation is owed to everybody. Neither concept, as such, is found in domestic law, although the domestic law principle of "ordre public" has a function similar to that of *jus cogens*. You may ask yourself why international law should set itself apart in this fashion. The reason is that the international system does not have a legislature. Norms are grown organically by the participants using treaties, custom and general principles of law, without any central coordination. Well-meaning lawyers, seeing the danger of complete contract autonomy, invented the concept of *jus cogens* and the obligation *erga omnes* in order to counteract the possibility of gross immorality, which would arise, for example, if the prohibition of genocide could be deviated from by agreement. Yet, both *jus cogens* and obligations *erga omnes* are poorly understood in jurisprudential thought, leading some even to question their existence. Others suggest that the fundamental norms of human rights have become *jus cogens* and are obligations *erga omnes*.

Unfortunately, the implication of an obligation *erga omnes* has not been well thought out. Part of the reason for this is the legacy of the famous German 19th century professor of international law, Heinrich Triepel, who proclaimed that the system of international law was separate from national legal systems. Triepel's theory became known as the dualist theory of international law, in contrast to the monist theory defined by those opposing Triepel's ideas. Although the sharp distinctions between dualist and monist thought have been much softened, Triepel has had lasting influence in his setting apart of international law; witness how that nation of lawyers, the United States, accepts that the "foreign question" doctrine puts most of the vital issues in international society beyond their reach. To the extent that the concept of *erga omnes* has been put into practice at all, it has been assumed, in the Triepel fashion, that *omnes* means all other States. The State owes an obligation to all other States to treat its own citizens well. It is hardly surprising that such a construct does not give rise to a wealth of international litigation, despite the masses of egregious violations occurring daily. Triepel's hand is visible in the concept because, in his view of the world, States can only owe an obligation to other States. A human right, a right of humans, becomes perverted into a right between States. In a rather twisted logic, this would not be so bad if it could then be assumed that the other States have a duty to protect the citizens of the first State. Yet, even where the human rights of a citizen of a State have been violated by another State, there is no duty for the state of origin to protect its citizen, only a right of "diplomatic protection". If one wants to be faithful to the idea behind *erga omnes*, one must leave behind the segmentation so poignantly defined by Triepel.

The obligation must be owed by everybody to everybody. And it must be invocable by everybody against everybody and even on behalf of somebody else!

This leaves us with a potentially litigational maze. If a Harvard law student could sue Exxon Mobil for funds to save starving children in Africa, would we not be entering a world without effective private ownership, one in which lives and corporations could be wrecked at will, serving only "ambulance chasers", and that only as long as they do not sue each other. The rebuttal of this is partly that *erga omnes* obligations only protect the most prized human attributes; but it must be admitted that, viewed that way, there is an uncanny likeness to a legal version of Peter Singer's marginal utility principle. We are therefore brought back to how legal process can encompass moral obligation. If the Harvard law student sues Exxon Mobil, one of the latter's defences could be that it has no commercial activity in the country in which the starvation is taking place. Logically, this would not get the company completely off the hook because the *erga omnes* obligation is owed by everybody to everybody. The absence of commercial activity in the country would mean, however, that Exxon Mobil should not be the one to foot the final bill. Exxon Mobil could rightly argue that its home state would be the more appropriate financier; Exxon Mobil could pass on the bill. Yet, Exxon Mobil's home state could possibly argue that it was not the right final destination either. In this fashion, the bill would continue to be passed on until it reached its rightful final destination, namely the country with the closest emotional proximity to the starving. Explaining it in this fashion, of course, makes it appear to be even more of an ambulance chaser's dream—endless chains of litigation endlessly reducing the proceeds available for the starving. But this is appearance only. Assuming an unrealistically quick and efficient legal system or, more realistically, a very persistent hunger crisis, the Harvard student would have achieved relief for the starving, albeit in a very inefficient manner, because Exxon Mobil would have had to pay up before it could pass on the bill. So the protection of the highest good, the human right, would have been achieved. The moral obligation of Exxon Mobil, coinciding with the legal obligation, could be said to have been to temporarily provide relief.

To accept the inconvenience of temporarily providing relief is not too much to ask when the reward would be to safeguard the highest human values. In practical terms, a comprehensive interpretation of the *erga omnes* obligation would not have draconian effects, however. There would always be the risk that the bill could not be passed on to the proper final recipient, but there would also always be the security that the bill could be passed on to the home state of the individual or corporation that had been forced to provide temporary relief, provided that the home state had a closer emotional proximity to the stricken population than the individual or corporation—something that would almost always be the case.

But when an element of the legal system is reinvented it also normally finds its feet again relatively quickly. The natural tendency would obviously be to directly sue the entity having the best possibility of providing relief and with the closest emotional proximity to the stricken population. The ambulance chaser would not necessarily get rich and secondary obligation would normally remain secondary.

In addition, people like Warren Buffett would soon offer "humanitarian aid insurance", thereby collectivizing the financial exposure. More importantly, however, litigation is an enforcement measure while the threat of litigation is a preventive measure. When we own up to our *erga omnes* obligations, and accept the threat of litigation at all levels, voluntary relief will come so much more readily. All we must do is to take seriously the fundamental rights of every human being. When we are serious we always dress our obligations in legal clothing without fearing litigative anarchy. That we did not do so in the past was due to a blind spot in our empathy, but with globalization, that blind spot has become unforgivable.

Yet, unforgivable as it might be, it is hard to avoid the thought that our lack of empathy might be explainable by inherent human features and hence that we are failing to comply with our *erga omnes* obligations simply because evolution has predisposed us for moral and legal failure. In a sense the most coherent explanation of the absence of substance of *erga omnes* obligations might be that our inherited view of the world is that our own genes are in eternal competition with the genes of others, and that therefore help to unrelated genes is counterproductive. Some flavours of group selection theory hold that we might be ready to sacrifice for others in our group, because our own genes to some extent will be present within the group, but that we are unwilling to sacrifice if no gene preservation purpose is served. Lemmings jump so that other lemmings may live—some of them with many of the genes of the suicidist. But lemmings do not jump to protect the elk. Whatever the validity of group selection theory, in pure logic it is, however, inconsistent that the lemming never jumps for the elk. In some situations the elk might be essential for the survival of lemmings, in terms of keeping down predators, in terms of keeping an ecological balance, and hence the advice to the lemming would sometimes have to be that it should sacrifice itself for the elk.

If you choose to believe in evolution as the only driver of development, you will conclude that many features of our social systems are premised on this broader logic that it serves the survival of our own genes to be compassionate. We help others through our social systems, because we cannot be sure that our offspring will not need help in the future in order to pass on our genes.

However, there is no reason to conclude that in an increasingly interconnected world evolutionary logic stops at the water's edge. In a twist on the "original position theory" of Rawls we should reason that we as the currently dominant tribes should help less fortunate tribes, because no dominance is eternal, and our offspring might need the help of the currently disfavoured tribes in the future in order to continue the passing-on of our genes.

"We do justice so that justice might be done to us in return" the saying goes. However, from an evolutionary standpoint it should say: "We help others pass on their genes, so that others in the future might help our genes to be passed on". So, evolutionary theory is not at all a bar to taking *erga omnes* obligations seriously. A mature forward looking human view of evolution dictates that we protect the lives of others, wherever they may be lived, in order to ensure in the best possible fashion that the lives of our own offspring are equally protected!

Chapter 4
The End Justifying the Means

Abstract The end justifying the means can be a terrifying concept, unless there is effective societal control. The concept is also based on a questionable distinction between means and ends. This notwithstanding, there are fundamental questions on what we as individuals or as a society should be willing to sacrifice in order to optimise individual or societal happiness. Proportionality remains the guide. Torture is clearly justified, even mandated, if the torture of one person can save the lives of a million. The issue becomes how to avoid sliding into abuse, and the solution might be by democratic oversight through the judiciary or supervisory committees. Yet, it is conceivable that the public is not ready to face the brutal reality sometimes justifying torture, and that, as a society, we are better off by closing our eyes and hoping that our leaders will be wise in the deployment. The other side of the coin is that the respect of the value of each individual dictates limits to what an individual can be forced to sacrifice. No human being should have to go into mortal combat against his will. If faced with extinction at least you must be asked!

Keywords The end justifying the means • Tao • Proportionality • Torture • Kant • Duty • Revolution • Terrorism • Cowardice • Pacifism • War

For a utilitarian it would seem easy to embrace the principle of 'the end justifying the means'. The principle reeks of proportionality, and the earlier discussions on *in dubio pro reo* and on whether a crime is always a crime are dyed in 'the end justifies the means' logic. Yet, in its pure form the principle introduces a wrongheaded proportionality, because it does not anchor the determination of the end in an objective or commonly agreed criterion.

With barebones 'the end justifies the means' we sink into Nietzsche's sea of moral relativism. "The end justifies the means" becomes an anarchist credo where there is no wrong and no right. Nietzsche is intuitively coupled with Machiavelli because in a valueless society there are no bounds to the principle that 'the end justifies the means'.

There is a tragic incongruity in the principle, as well. In a results-oriented world we are conditioned to believe that the end is, indeed, an end. Yet, the only end in a human life is death; all other ends are steps in a process. The same is true

P. Hulsroj, *The Principle of Proportionality*, SpringerBriefs in Law,
DOI: 10.1007/978-94-007-5775-2_4, © The Author(s) 2013

for society in general. Apart from nuclear obliteration, society never reaches an end point, it only moves from one achievement or one disaster to another. If there is no end of any significant finality we must reject any general notion that ends can justify any means.

A human life is a process, is Tao. A society progresses through a dynamic process, no less a Tao. Our lives are hence dominated by a dynamic in which means often occupy a larger role than ends and where means and ends often become inseparable. Is the important thing about winning Wimbledon, that by doing so you become a 'Wimbledon winner' enjoying the respect of your peers until the end of your time? Or is the important thing about winning Wimbledon the experience you have in doing so, and reminiscing about that experience? If the price of becoming a Wimbledon winner would be that all memory of your tennis playing would be erased would you choose that rather than hold on to all your memories of your tennis Tao, even if nobody would remember your exalted status as a Wimbledon winner?

The Germans say that *Der Weg is das Ziel*, the journey is the destination. This is largely true, but should not be understood to mean that a life dominated by the path must be, or should be, a life without values. The path we live is obviously influenced by the sum of the 'ends' we achieve. A life with a full belly is immeasurably better than one with an empty one; it might be better to be the king and not the pauper.

In our individual lives this means that we have a constant stream of value judgments to make. How much of process comfort am I ready to give up for a given end that might provide me greater satisfaction thereafter? As a moral human being how much of my means am I ready to give up to serve a laudable societal end?

As long as both ends and means are within your control and raise no legal or moral questions, the value trade-offs you make is your business, is part of your self-determination. But when the means you want to deploy involve sacrifice by others or when society starts to pursue ends at your cost you get to value trade-offs that can become entirely unhinged, because we believe that ends are, indeed, ends and means, indeed, means.

The important point is this: for an end to justify a means, the end must be removed from the realm of the subjective. Democracy is our standard tool in this respect, although, in truth, democracy is no more than compounded subjectivity. Still, compounded subjectivity is a step in the direction of objectivisation, notwithstanding the many means that have been so cruelly sacrificed on the altar of democratically endorsed but tragically wrong ends.

For a utilitarian it is true that building society is all about subjecting means to ends, but through democratic control. And for a utilitarian it is certainly true that what you give up in comfort in order to achieve a result must be measured against the comfort provided by the result. The first three chapters intended to show that in a comfort trade-off it is logical to slacken the rigours of *in dubio pro reo*, to allow some crimes not to be crimes and to institutionalise being a good neighbour, but this is a logic that is presented to the sovereign, the people, for adoption through the democratic process; these are not self-service concepts.

4.1 Ends, Means and the Dangers of Self-Service

The ideological roots of terrorism are in revolution. Romantic justification of revolution centres on a vague concept of self-defence. And since self-defence has a strong element of proportionality it would seem that a beautiful circle is closed in which terrorism is justified by proportionality and by the perennial clamouring about ends justifying means.

The legal rigour of Hans Kelsen's thinking made him adverse to the concept of revolution, and there are good reasons to be sceptical as long as you stay in the legal universe. However, revolution is, of course, by definition, an extra-juridical event and should hence not excite the lawyers too much. The sad truth, from a legal perspective, is that a failed revolution is a crime, a successful revolution an indictment of the previous regime as criminal. Neither history nor law can lay claim to absolute truth, and certainly law is well advised to stay within its systemic reference frame. A failed revolution is a crime, which, of course, does not go to say that a failed revolution was morally indefensible. However, the great thing about revolution is that, Castro's small band of comrades apart, it requires a popular backing to become successful. So there is a sort of informal democratic control in revolution.

But also revolution tends either to be quickly successful or quickly fail. Hence, revolution does not normally bring societal instability of long duration, although it might be the result thereof. Revolution does not endanger the Tao, the daily life comfort, in the way terrorism does.

In Chap. 2 it was argued that a crime is not a crime if its commission brings a much larger individual benefit. A terrorist would argue that his acts follow the same logic. The terrorist sacrifices innocent life in order to bring about a much bigger benefit to other innocent lives. Yet, the terrorist logic fails not only because it escapes 'democratic control', judicial control and extracts a high toll on the Tao of ordinary citizens who are led to live in fear. It fails relative to the logic of Chap. 2 because there is no direct link, no direct proportionality between act and benefit. When the bank is robbed in order to provide life saving surgery the crime is exculpated only if the robbery was necessary to get the surgery. The terrorist invests crime in the hope that ultimately perceived societal benefits will arise. But this remains hope only. The link between crime and expected benefit rests not only on subjectivity, but on predictions that history has shown are overwhelmingly wrong. Democratic consensus is that the few societal benefits terrorism might have occasioned throughout history are by far outweighed by its historical cost. Revolution is another matter!

4.2 Kant, Means and End

If one takes at face value Kant's dictum on the unacceptability of treating the human being as a means rather than an end one gets to the extreme position of Nozick or beyond. One gets to the antithesis of utilitarianism. Yet, Kant's noble enlightenment should not be understood as more than an exhortation to respect the value of individuals. In our modern society where means and ends are often hard to distinguish and where ends might be sacrificed on the altar of the means as readily as means on the altar of ends, every human is a prioritised asset, but prioritised both individually and as part of a collectivity.

The tension between the value of a human being as an individual and the value of a multitude of individuals, all of equal value, plays out very palpably in the debates about the admissibility of torture. Our vision in this respect becomes blurred by the inhumanity and vulgarity of Abu Ghraib and by unresolved issues on the governance of torture. Yet, from a moral perspective there is no complication. Only a fool would abstain from torture if the torture of one human being could save the lives of a million.

In fact, George Bernhard Shaw gave us the logic long ago when he asked an attractive woman whether she would go to bed with him for a thousand pounds and continued upping the price until she equivocated. He then asked her if she would go to bed with him for five pounds, to which she indignantly answered: "What do you take me for!" "We have already established what you are", Shaw replied. "Now we are merely haggling over the price". In the same vein, we are all torturers and what we should be haggling about is the 'price' of torture, that is, when are the benefits of torture so great as to justify it, and, importantly, how do we manage torture?

Conceivably, it is better to be in denial about the possible necessity of torture or perhaps it is better to control its use by oversight committees—or by the judiciary as proposed by Alan Dershowitz.[1] Yet, President Obama was eloquently wrong when he said in his inauguration speech: 'As for our common defense, we reject as false the choice between our safety and our ideals. Our founding fathers… our founding fathers, faced with perils we can scarcely imagine, drafted a charter to assure the rule of law and the rights of man, a charter expanded by the blood of generations. Those ideals still light the world, and we will not give them up for expedience's sake'.

For torture there is sadly a choice to be made between our ideals of respect for each individual and our ideals to protect the value of our collectivity of individuals, each of equal value. The question is not one of 'expedience' and this is surely understood by the commander in chief of two wars in which innocent human beings constantly died, as collateral damage, without fair trial and respect for individual value.

Still, perhaps it is better to be in denial! Perhaps it is better to be discrete about how it would be morally repugnant to refuse the use of torture when its use would bring overwhelming benefit. Perhaps the public is not ready to face this most brutal of realities.

Yet, denial and window-dressing do not alter the fundamental truth that if you prioritise human value then sometimes you are morally obliged to expend it in order to protect even greater human value. Torture is sometimes a categorical imperative!

---

[1] Want to Torture? Get a Warrant. San Francisco Chronicle, 22 January 2002.

4.3 Kant and Cowardice

There is something profoundly touching in the master of duty putting the human being as an end rather than a means. Yet, Kant did not see a dichotomy between human beings as ends and their duty to occupy the battlefield, his preference for militias notwithstanding. In fact, even the most ardent rejecters of utilitarianism have had little hesitation in endorsing the obligation to wager one's life on the fields of honour. Similarly, pacifism is normally based on broad moral or pragmatic considerations, but rarely sees the use of soldiers as means to an end as opposable in itself. Pragmatic pacifists tend to see war as an ineffective tool towards any noble end, not as something inherently wrong because it instrumentalises the human being.

In Marxism the proletariat as a means of production can be used also as a means towards its own end of dictatorship and can hence be used as the means for war. Not surprising, perhaps, for a collectivist and largely utilitarian philosophy, yet utterly disturbing when the idea is to avoid the abuse of the means of production. To become cannon fodder in order to break one's own chains of slavery introduces more than a little tension into the equation, and it can be argued that this disrespect for individual life was the seed that ultimately made the communist project collapse. Kant would have seen his enlightenment humanism proven right, in the sense that the chain of thought that downplays individual value will ultimately ignore individual human value. This is a charge that could also be levelled at utilitarianism, and is the starting point for Nozick's ultra-liberalism. Yet, there is peril in both extremes, that of the pure collectivism and that of pure individualism. The risk of pure individualism is that it refuses to enlarge the cake, merely because the only way to meaningfully enlarge the cake is through collaboration. If you refuse taxes to fund roads you will not drive! Eventually we are back to the Aristotelian balance of the appetites: too far in one direction, you fail, too far in the other, you fail.

So evidently a society must be based on individual respect of a certain number of general obligations, put in place to increase the commonwealth. Where the balance is to be found between rules and freedom is a continuous quest with no absolute answer at any given time, valid for all given societies.

Still, a Kantian question remains of whether there is an outer boundary for what a human being can be compelled to do or sacrifice.

Godwin posed the question of whether the son should save the archbishop of Cambrai or his mother. You could take this question one step further and ask whether you could be forced to sacrifice your heart so that an eminent physician could get himself a heart transplant, allowing him to continue his research which would ultimately save hundreds of lives. The dilemma of the Godwin question changes subtly. You do not have to choose between your loved one and a most useful one, but society has to choose between you and a most useful one. When put in this fashion we would all, correctly, answer that society cannot have the right to make such a choice. And our logic is ultimately Kantian: no human being can, to such an extent, be made a means to an end.

Words and perceptions are deceptive, however. The difference between the transplant example and the situation in which a soldier is sent to certain death in battle is only distinguishable by the fact that the sacrifice of the life of the soldier is much less certain to bring benefit than society forcing you to sacrifice your heart to save the eminent physician.

If there is a kernel of truth in Kant's perspective on means versus ends then it is that no human being should be forced to sacrifice his life, or put it at high risk, for some greater good, not endorsed by this human being himself as being worthy of his sacrifice.

It is sadly a beautiful myth only that each human being is a master of his fate, captain of his soul. Even so, not to have the right to be asked to make the ultimate sacrifice, human existence, but to be instructed to make it, is antithetical to human existence itself.

If society wants your life, if it wants to send you into mortal combat, at least it must be obliged to ask!

Chapter 5
True Globalisation

Abstract The foundation of globalisation is liberal economics and the concept is propagated by the American-led 1 %. Globalisation is a permutation of empire, and this one is far less inclusive than it should be. This is problematic because the durability of empire tends to be predicated on inclusiveness—take the example of the Romans. The British empire failed largely because is was discriminatory and non-inclusive, although heeding the call for representation as a function of taxation could have yielded a truly communal structure, and thus given lie to the current quasi-religious attachment to sovereignty. The United States still has the possibility to expand its reach, not only virtually but territorially, for instance, by seeking to create a federation of federations with Mexico and Canada. The industrialised world can also defend empire by becoming more inclusive and allow far more immigration of the lesser skilled. The logic of Adam Smith dictates not only production where it is most advantageous, but also free mobility of labour. That this would overwhelm the West is a myth!

Keywords Empire • Immigration • Borders • The 1 % • Values • Adam Smith • Sovereignty • Globalisation • 'No taxation without representation' • Proportionality • Free movement of labour

Empires are born and die. Lifetimes might differ, but imperial domination is as cyclical as the capitalist boom and bust cycles of Marx. Tony Blair reminded the US Congress of this reality in a rousing speech in 2007, and left it as an unalterable fact. Empires rule proportional to vitality; when vitality ebbs Empire weakens. Yet modern economics have moderated the capitalist boom and bust cycles. The cyclical nature of economic activity has not been eliminated, but peaks and troughs have become less extreme, the current crisis notwithstanding. A crucial question is whether imperial cycles can be managed similarly.

Empire's characteristic is the dominance by one group of many other groups. The present liberal democracy empire spearheaded by the one billion of the First World has assured untold material and non-material wealth for First World citizens and has in recent decades brought increased prosperity also for most other regions of the world, with large parts of Africa being the glaring exception.

P. Hulsroj, *The Principle of Proportionality*, SpringerBriefs in Law,
DOI: 10.1007/978-94-007-5775-2_5, © The Author(s) 2013

A popular theory postulates that the globalisation element of the liberal democracy empire has created a new global elite, chosen through meritocracy and without regard to nationality. The masters of the financial world are the key constituents of this new global elite. The upshot of this theory is that First World Empire is being replaced by a basically exploitative elite creating its own empire dissociated from country and nationality. In a sense this may be a naive dream. If one follows the logic to its ultimate consequence then it would mean that a global elite would eventually create a world without boundaries, where humans would be rewarded in proportion to talent not according to birthright or nationality. Yet, since this postulated global elite operates on the maxim of minimum government, it is not clear that meritocracy across all strata of the global society will follow, and, indeed, it is not clear at all that this global elite has waved nationality goodbye. An American Master of the Universe is still mostly very American, and Chinese tycoons are certainly very Chinese.

This notwithstanding, there is a fundamental question of whether the linkage between empire and nation can be broken and replaced by a link between individual ability and power; of whether the inevitable social strata of society can really be globalised far beyond what is the case now for the global financial elite. The first obstacle for this is the high impermeability of borders.

5.1 Borders

The raison d'être of borders is protectionism. In popular mythology it is held that borders serve to keep out possible immigrants whose only intention is to abuse the social support system of the target country. This is only a very small part of the story, however. The main purpose of borders is to protect the labour force of a country against competition from less wealthy immigrants. Globalisation tends to hail the free movement of goods, witness the WTO, and thus heeds Adam Smith's dogma that goods should be produced where it is most efficient to do so. Yet the logic of Adam Smith would normally dictate that goods should not only be produced where it is most efficient, but also that labour should be deployed where it can be most efficient. Borders thus prevent rational implementation of Adam Smith, but also belie the credo of globalisation, where efficiency is supposed to be the only operating parameter.

The free mobility of labour within the EU or the long-standing mobility within the US are professions of faith in the efficiency of letting labour move where it can be best deployed and are testaments to the very real gains that accrue. Yet global labour is generally segmented horizontally and vertically. Each nation competes against all other nations and, within each nation, each social class competes against all other social classes.

Much has been made of how the horizontal segmentation of India's caste system has kept back the material progress of the sub-continent. Less is said about the vertical segmentation system of nations that creates similar inefficiencies and that neither in origin nor in effect and cruelty differs substantially from the caste system.

Efficiency is sought by moving suitable production to the most auspicious labour location, instead of letting labour coalesce in the place where boundary conditions are the most favourable. The explosion of container shipping is a demonstration both of the efficiency and the inefficiency of the labour market. Sometimes production is, indeed, better done away from the place of consumption, sometimes it would have been better to produce close to the consumer. The vertical segmentation limits the efficiency choice, but also conveniently obscures salary inequality and its consequences.

5.2 Common Culture and Political Institutions

Political institutions and common culture do not necessarily go hand in hand. One can speculate, as Francis Fukuyama does,[1] on what comes first, but regardless of the answer one can conclude that political institutions might be passed on to new regimes, without the common culture with which these institutions may have been associated being passed on as well. And conversely, the culture of a society might be passed on without related institutions. This does not go to say that there is no connection between culture and political institutions, it would be difficult to imagine the Western anarchic cultural scene develop within an authoritarian system, but once developed the possibility of independent life of culture and political institutions is a possibility. Greek culture lived on strongly even within the much more rigorous institutional setting of the Romans. Yet, the link between culture and institutional set-up is strong, particularly in the domain of political culture. The human rights defined during the French Revolution dictated a certain institutional approach, and it was the tragedy of the French Revolution that this was not understood or respected by its leaders. A humanistic society cannot be created by inhuman means no matter what Robespierre, Marx and Mao might have argued. The human rights defined in the UN human rights covenants dictate a certain institutional setting, since some of the rights are institutional themselves, such as the right to vote or the right to education.

If the European and American centuries have treasured human rights and if the West sees human rights as a universal good to be preserved even when the West's dominance recedes, the question becomes whether this is possible given the strong link between the human rights culture and the attendant institutions.

Dawkins has in an almost comically self-indulgent way suggested that ideas develop in a pattern similar to evolutionary biology. It is, however, questionable whether there is more merit to this logic than there was to Herbert Spencer's

[1] The origins of political order.

social Darwinism. Ideas no not combine and mutate in the random fashion of genes, and selection is deliberate, not just a question of objective efficiency in a given environmental frame as in evolutionary biology. Still, it is obviously true that a significant element in the survival of ideas is whether they survive in the competition of ideas. History has known long dormant periods of viable ideas, lying in wait for the right societal circumstances, whilst being suppressed by hostile forces that have ultimately been defeated either in the arena of the competition of ideas or in the more brutal world of Realpolitik. The sad truth is that new regimes look at ideas only from the perspective of their utility for their, possibly unsavoury, purposes, not from the perspective of whether the ideas are good from an individualistic or broader societal perspective. The short term prospect of humanistic ideas is not always that rosy.

5.3 Empire, Commonwealth, and the Lost Opportunity

Inclusiveness is an important element in the longevity of empires. The Roman Empire lasted for so long partly because it made possible that so many became Romans. The granting of citizenship was a reward for non-Romans and Roman/non-Roman marriages expanded citizenship considerably over the generations.

The last of the territorially based empires, the British, dug its own grave by being so extra-ordinarily non-inclusive. The demand of the colonialists in the New World was for representation in Parliament, and had it been granted the Boston Tea Party would have been no party at all. Of course, some Britons understood the necessity of inclusiveness, understood 'no taxation without representation'. Hence eminent ones led by William Pitt the Elder supported the American demand for representation in Parliament and, indeed, suggested that Parliament should consist of representatives from America, the West Indies and Ireland alongside the British parliamentarians. Imagine what thus could have happened in the middle of the 18th century and how subsequently Canada, South Africa, Australia and ultimately India might have gained representation as a logical consequence of William Pitt's argument. Many conflicts would have been avoided, perhaps replaced by others, equally insoluble, but the kernel of a potentially egalitarian global governance structure could have been established. The 'empire' as a federal structure with true representation is a thought to behold, instead we got messy, poverty sustaining de-colonisation, through which helpless indigenous populations more often than not were exposed to rapine by indigenous, unscrupulous elites with little preparation for good governance or government but with as greedy hearts as the colonial masters before them. After the end of WWII the time had passed for a federal commonwealth, but imagine again that the empire had been inclusive and had become a federal structure. How much better the world would have been off, even if national independence movements might have meant that the structure would have broken up after WWII! Indeed, neither WWI nor WWII would have taken place in the way they did if Britain had not been seen as weakened; would not have taken place in this form if the empire had been a federal structure based on equality. The colonists of America wanted to be English like the English—and the English would not let them! It was a historical opportunity lost and it was, in a sense, surprising considering that the English after much bloodshed had created the union with Scotland and that this had been a much-sought prize. Perhaps English stupidity in Ireland led to the stupidity in America, but that makes neither Ireland nor America less of a lost opportunity.

5.4 The Inclusiveness of the Virtual Empire

Let there be no doubt about it. We are living through the later phase of an American empire. It started in 1917 when Europe could not settle its business without American help, it grew during WWII, accelerated in the 50s and early 60s, and reached its pinnacle in the 80 and 90s. Despite Vietnam and the messiness of Iraq and Afghanistan, it is a subtle empire, non-territorial, and driven by economic might, liberal economics and the moral high ground of liberal democracy. Because of the heterogeneous population of the United States and the related immigration culture it has been more inclusive than most, and WASP culture has made Europe feel very much at home.

The postulate that economic might is at the core of the American virtual empire might be questioned, of course. English as the lingua franca would seem to point to culture as a pillar, as well as the large number of prominent American authors. Few non-American movies become global hits. Yet, the American empire starts and ends with economic power. For three hundred years the beauty of Shakespeare's English did not make English the lingua franca. American English is the language of money, of technology, Anglo-English is the language of culture and understated emotion. Many American movies are, in fact, British and for every Humphrey Bogart there is a Laurence Olivier.

Science and technology is obviously an American stronghold and one can discuss whether this prowess is the foundation of economic might or the other way round. A pointless discussion, in fact, since the reality is that economic might and scientific and technological capability go hand in hand, are mutually reinforcing—a lesson well learned by the new Asian powerhouses, but sadly ignored in a lip-syncing, but paralysed Europe.

5.5 Europe and the Empire

One of the glorious things about the American empire is that many of its subjects only vaguely recognise their fealty. The comic British references to 'the special relationship' try to mask inequality and Gallic pride may satisfy a soul that nevertheless and despite protestations is becoming more and more American. Only a few years ago the French sought to teach the world about the virtues of the French type of capitalism, now Europe has learned that it is in the American slipstream no matter what it proclaims—and that Europe is even less capable of steering through an economic downturn than a not overly impressive United States. Max Weber memorably wrote about The Protestant Ethic and the Spirit of Capitalism and the Germans, having also hosted American troops for more than 50 years, might be the most clear-eyed on what drives America and the world and might hence have been able to create the most successful fusion of American and European values, yet also Germany is, of course, much helped by its economic might, based on science and technology just as in the United States. It is interesting that a country like Germany, so chock-full of intellectualism, is, at the same time able to be so economically successful. Germany is not America, but the parallels are so striking that, paradoxically, neither Germany nor the United States truly realise.

In the final analysis, Europe is an enabler of the American virtual empire. The beauty of virtualness is that the empire can be sold in different flavours. When American rhetoric becomes too crass, softer European voices can convey the message to reluctant newer vassals and keep them within the province of liberal economics. The opening of new markets has made great wealth possible not only in the heartland of materialism, America, but also for its allies, and in this sense the American empire has been genuinely inclusive. Yet, liberal economics have little sentimentality and will not forever smile at its favourite son. Asia awaits and Confucius will not be in the way. The pupil will become the master.

5.6 Brain Drain

The inclusiveness of an empire is to a large extent defined by the access to the elite for foreigners. The Ottoman Empire was built around its Janissary class of Christian origin administrators and warriors drawn from the outer provinces, yet this was hardly an inclusive system, since the whole effort was to make the Janissaries dependent only on the sultan. All links to family, original religion or region were erased as thoroughly as possible and the status could not be passed on to progeny.

Other empires have been less cruel in allowing foreigners into their elites. Rome made talented foreigners Romans and they could rise to the very top, as the example of Emperor Macrinus and others shows. The Habsburg empire was not nationality based in the first place, but revolved around the dynastic ambitions of the Habsburg family, and hence the elite was always multinational and extraordinarily inclusive. Although territory, in various configurations, defined the Habsburg empire this family enterprise was the first to draw very indiscriminately on the talent pool, and thus the empire was built and kept together without resort to national sentiment.[2] The loyalty that was built was towards the empire and its rulers.

[2] A.J.P. Taylor, The Habsburg monarchy.

The culture of the American empire was for a long time strongly rooted in its history of being a refuge, a country of immigration. Despite the Native- and African-American experience, it was inclusive almost by definition. A WASP background might have been helpful, but 'the pursuit of happiness' was understood to be able to bring people of most ethnic backgrounds into the elite. Recent decades have been a mixed bag, as the empire has broken down internal barriers (Jews, Catholics, Native Americans, Afro-Americans, women), whilst building higher and higher barriers towards the outside. The brain drain has become very selective. And yet the United States continues to attract an impressive amount of talent. However, the real inclusiveness of America's empire is due to its being virtual, due to it being a trade and capital empire, allowing vassals of all stripes, and their subjects, to enter the US managed elite, provided they can trade well or allocate capital well. The American empire is as indiscriminate in allowing entry into the elite as Habsburg, only the United States has dispensed entirely with territory. The American empire is in the final analysis a coalition of the willing, and, on the face of it, geography plays little role, since the United States has had the critical mass to preserve and protect its dominance. The 1 % demonised by Occupy Wall Street has replaced the Habsburgs as the owners of empire, has perfected the Habsburg model by way of Adam Smith.

5.7 So Location does not Matter?

For the top performers within each national liberal economy, indeed, geography is of little import. The absolute elites of each country tied-into America's empire circulate quite freely and a Chinese billionaire does not need to be in the United States to earn his billions. In many cases too high mobility of the 1 % might be counterproductive for wealth generation. Chinese and Russian billions must normally be made by persons who have retained a very strong link to the countries from which they source their wealth.

Although, as mentioned above, American billionaires remain very much American and Chinese ones remain Chinese, it is equally true that American and Chinese billionaires in a cultural sense share more than an American billionaire shares with an American assembly line worker, or a Chinese billionaire shares with a Chinese peasant. Amongst billionaires of a certain nationality, there is obviously a shared cultural hinterland that fosters solidarity, yet most would abandon nationality in two shakes of a lamb's tail if given the choice between nationality and wealth. The 'Paris is well worth a Mass' of Henry IV is equally valid for most wealthy people, no matter their protestations of patriotism. Upbringing is, of course, an ineradicable shaper of personality, and hence one may argue that an American remains an American 'by any other name'. The basic point on nationality is, however, Darwinian. American wealthy people will prefer more wealthy Americans essentially because it increases the chances that their offspring will also live in wealth, since statistically mono-nationality marriages are still prevalent. If marriage became predominantly wealth based rather than nationality based, we would be likely to see the wealth based elite increasingly waving goodbye to nationality as tribal marking, just as the aristocracy has done for centuries. Nationality might have remained relevant as a source of wealth for the aristocracy, and might also remain so for the wealth elite for a long time to come, but for marriage it was more important to be noble than to be of the same nationality.

The fault line in all of this, particularly in a virtual empire, is the ever decreasing solidarity between social classes within nations. The welfare states of Western Europe are premised on social solidarity, perhaps for ethical reasons, but also for Darwinian ones; when most are well taken care of the likelihood of offspring also being well taken care of is big. Americans are, amazingly, more a people of gamblers in this respect. Rapid ascent and rapid descent are always a distinct possibility. There are many conditioning factors in this, the most important one being the constitutionally enshrined unrealistic optimism that the right to the pursuit of happiness will indeed lead to happiness. A more evolved Darwinian perspective would logically lead to the welfare state.

But that is not where we are now! The virtual American empire measures its wealth in overall GDP, and cares nothing about the distribution of wealth. It is a miracle that the impoverishing of the middle and working classes has not yet led to serious social action (but watch Occupy Wall Street as a symbol of discontent) and it is tragic that the enemy of the American worker is the Chinese worker, rather than the American billionaire who wants to lower his taxes and who sponges off both the American and the Chinese worker. There was an impeccable logic to the Socialist Internationale, a logic that has been turned on its head by the creation of a less structured, but much stronger, Capitalist Internationale.

5.8 Grow, Grow!

The commonly accepted theory in management is that when a company stops growing it starts failing. This is highly debatable, since it might be perfectly respectable for a company to say that it has reached its limit, or steady state, and to seek to manage that situation, and perhaps allow a gradual decline managed to optimise benefits for the share- and stakeholders of having reached a peak and having to slowly descend. Seeking to optimise the benefits of a logical decline is certainly better than to desperately try to continue growing beyond natural limitations—and ultimately experience Schumpeter's creative destruction as Kodak recently did.

Translated into empire, management theory should mean that the American empire will start to fade when it no longer grows. And this will in all likelihood be true. Empire is eclipsed by other empire, just as company is eclipsed by other company. Now, there are a few areas where liberal capitalism still has to take hold, and hence the American virtual empire has not yet run its course. Yet, the United Stated has another option for growing which used to be in its playbook, but which has now been forgotten because of the convenience of virtual empire, and that is, physical empire. Ever since Hawaii became the 50th state in 1959 the United States has ceased growing physically, although Puerto Rico is obvious for statehood, for instance. This lack of growth is perhaps the most telltale sign of decline. Much derided Europe has grown increasingly together 'physically' while the United States has grown its virtual empire only. Yet, the United States has not reached its limits, and can be argued to withhold wealth, and diminish its own wealth, by stopping the building of physical empire before time, based on entirely xenophobic reasons, or based on time-honoured principles which time has thrown aside. The Monroe Doctrine is not as valid as it was.

Within an entirely democratic setting the United States could obviously offer the population of Mexico the prospect of constituting the next five or six states of the Union. This sounds preposterous, but is not. Mexico is not a failed state but it is a state with tremendous problems, some of them stemming from Mexico's proximity to the United States, many of them home-grown governance issues. Building a Fortress America to stem the tide of Mexican immigrants seeking their fortune in the Promised Land is both inhuman and counterproductive for American and Mexican wealth. The United States might in the past have been deterred by anti-colonialist sentiment from expanding, and rightly so, but surely there can be nothing wrong in seeking union by means of the ballot box. US racism towards Latinos will be a big obstacle, nonsensical arguments about the language barrier as well (although the US is already bi-lingual in many respects, and Europe has shown that the language barrier is not insurmountable), and Mexican pride and patriotism might make this appear as Utopian as a supra-national structure tying together century-old enemies like France, Germany and United Kingdom would have appeared in the 1920s.

Clearly, a broader based United States would not be built overnight. NAFTA was a nice timid step, and upon that more and more integration should be built, ultimately bringing more and more trade and more and more mobility of the workforce. And perhaps the ultimate destination should rather be a federation of federal states, the Union of American States, allowing the wealthier and more stand-offish Canada to be brought in as well. This would create a truly North American polity and eliminate the absurdity of Alaska being so separate from the rest of the United States. A federation of federations of 450 million citizens would be something to behold—almost as big as the European Union!

5.9 The Free Mobility of Labour

There is, of course, a more fundamental question of mobility than just the one associated with the border between the United States and Mexico. The violence there and the despair of the boat people trying to gain entry to the European Union from the south are but symptoms of a broader malaise that the American virtual empire must address or it will vanish.

As discussed earlier, borders are very permeable for the 1 %, and they are somewhat permeable for the brain drain relevant ones, but almost impermeable for the lower skilled. Given the impotence of the lower skilled the lack of mobility might appear not to be a challenge for the American virtual empire—but it is. It is also a disgrace and, as discussed, entirely against the patron saint, Adam Smith. The fear related to global mobility of labour is, of course, that billions of Asians and Africans will land on Western shores, will bankrupt our social systems and drive us from comfort to despondency. Yet, our fears are overblown and much depends on how such mobility would be introduced and managed.

The first measure the masters of empire should introduce should be decent living conditions globally. This is obviously easier said than done. Many of the GATT and WTO trade rounds have stumbled over the issue of minimum wages in developing countries—sadly for the entirely wrong reasons. For the industrialised countries to insist on minimum wages in order to protect their own industry is immoral, to say the least. If industrialised countries had set up an off-setting fund it would have made sense, however. In other words, if developing countries had been compensated for the difference between actual earning power and a decent salary it would have been good, since the competitiveness of exports from developing countries would have been safeguarded. Clearly, our idealism is not strong enough for this, but it should be a non-sequitur that exports from developing countries should never be subject to customs duties. Developing countries at least deserve a level playing field with domestic industry in industrialised counties. That would be the first dictate of Adam Smith! But also a first reason why emigration would be far less than paranoia would imply.

In any event mobility requires the ability to move, and the vast majority of destitute populations do not have the logistical means or mental preparedness to move away from the local environment. The move from the countryside to the city is a fact of life in all emerging economies, but moving to another country involves other kinds of barriers altogether, including language. Thus, another element meaning that paranoid nightmares would not come true.

A less appealing control measure could be to sell immigration rights. The argument that could be made in favour of this is that the population of a given country inherits a certain infrastructure, which others should only be able to enjoy if they pay for the right to share in the inheritance. The poor immigrant would be saddled with a debt upon entry, which he would have to gradually pay off. Such a system, which has a certain economic logic, would obviously mean that the wealth trade-off for the prospective immigrant would be significantly weighted down, and the attraction of emigration would decrease. It appears inhuman, but is less inhuman than keeping immigrants completely out. It would increase permeability.

But then there is the point of the drowning of social security systems. Now, it is a fact that no country is obliged to extend full social benefits to non-citizens, but it is equally a fact that it is impermissible to have human beings dying from hunger in the streets of a welfare state. Yet, immigration can be linked to having work and not being a burden for the state, meaning that an immigrant can be deported if not working. In most countries the status of permanent resident protects against such deportation, but entry to a country on a non-permanent resident basis, and the permission to work, mostly has as a corollary the obligation to leave when no longer working or able to sustain oneself. Broadening this to deal with a potentially large number of non-permanent immigrants might again be inhuman, but better than closed borders.

The upshot of this is that there are many ways to avoid unmanageable immigration, but only one way to optimise imperial welfare growth and to avoid the crumbling of empire, and that is to open borders, or at least to open them far more, and to more classes of labour!

Chapter 6
Large and Small Crimes

Abstract Societies have over the centuries been more focused on stamping out micro crimes than macro such. Theft and murder have been reined in through the criminal systems, but only with the Statute of the International Criminal Court did we start to make a real effort to criminalise gross governmental malfeasance. Yet there is a long way to go in this domain. The likely cooking of the books by Greece to gain entry to the Euro has not been investigated, let alone prosecuted, although this would have been the first action had large banks been doing the damage. The raping of entire countries, like by Mugabe in Zimbabwe, is not outlawed, and not much frowned upon. In a generation's time hopefully the embryo constituted by the Statute of the International Criminal Court has developed into a comprehensive set of norms regulating what is acceptable behaviour by our rulers, and given rise to an intervention, criminal sanction and enforcement system at the international level. And much before then hopefully we will have outlawed that politicians lie to us, and created national institutions monitoring veracity and sanctioning mendacity.

Keywords International crime • Public crimes • Statute of the international criminal court • Politicians lying • Cooking of the books • Proportionality • Sovereignty • Sanctions • Responsibility to protect • Global charter • Political question doctrine

In assessing our societal order, an anthropologist from another planet would have great difficulty understanding the prioritisation of our system of sanctions.

Small crimes, murder, theft, fraud, are punished severely and have been so for centuries, whilst large crimes, genocide, the starting of war, were criminalised only recently and still often go unpunished. The rape of entire countries by their rulers is neither criminalised on the international level nor much frowned upon.

Historically this might be understandable. When progressing from 'the state of nature' the first step must always be to reign in private malfeasance, to avoid that one human being kills another human being. And historically even the Peace of Westphalia, with its legitimisation of war as a political tool, might be understandable. As humanity emerged from the darkness of the Middle Ages, and the

P. Hulsroj, *The Principle of Proportionality*, SpringerBriefs in Law,
DOI: 10.1007/978-94-007-5775-2_6, © The Author(s) 2013

fierce fight for individual and collective survival, it might not have been seen as strange to reflect the lived reality in an instrument of peace, although this instrument of peace became an exculpator of immense bloodshed for two and a half centuries.

Yet, almost a century after the Briand Kellogg Pact rescinded Westphalia we have still not succeeded entirely in raising our gaze from private to public crime. Many encouraging developments have taken place, starting with the Versailles Treaty seeking to put Wilhelm II on trial, to the League of Nations, the Nuremberg trials, the Charter of the United Nations, and recently the Statute of the International Criminal Court, yet we are still lacking in the appraisal of many macro-crimes, in delegitimizing and punishing them. Our measure of proportionality still often fails where it concerns the grossest of violations; often fails in the economic area and when perpetrators carry the cloak of officialdom.

6.1 Private and Public Crimes

A very good peace-time illustration of the divide between micro and macro crimes is provided by the Euro financial crisis. The trigger of the crisis was the precarious state of the Greek economy. Yet, the precarious state of the Greek economy should have meant that Greece should not have gained entry to the Euro. And it seems clear that Greece only succeeded in doing so by cooking its books then and for years thereafter.

What is truly remarkable is that nobody has shown any interest in the individual responsibility for the cooking of the books. Europe, and the European project, has suffered mightily from the behaviour of Greece, and Portugal and Spain are facing almost unbearable hardship because of the Greek contagion. If this had been the work of large investment banks surely heads would have rolled, but because it was the work of government employees nobody looks in their direction. Macro public crimes go unpunished, where micro private crimes with the same topology in terms of effect and suffering are met with the burning sword. The macro crimes in Greece have led to billions of losses for private investors holding Greek public bonds, so even if one argued that states lying to other states is the order of the day, and that there was a degree of inter-state complicity, then lying to private investors is normally sacrilege. It may be that political elites are not so keen on exposing other political elites because lying has become accepted practice. Yet, the reason private investors, and the public at large, allow such malfeasance to go un-investigated and unpunished is because our conditioning is still very much that the "King can do no wrong" and that governmental and sovereign privilege are seen as unassailable.

The Statute of the International Criminal Court operates on a subsidiarity principle because enforcement is normally better when effected on the domestic level. In this vein it would have been salutary to have seen Greek institutions investigate the fiddlers of the books on their own initiative, but it might be understandable why this has not been the case. What is not understandable is that the other European states did not make it a condition for bail-outs that proper investigation and, as relevant, prosecution would be undertaken. One might take the lofty view that revenge is of no interest, but the fact is that without investigation we will not learn enough from this disaster, and without prosecution no deterrent for the future will have been achieved. And if prosecution should show that no crime was committed, we will have no chance to introduce the proper penal provisions to signal that in the future such macro crimes will be intolerable.

Is it necessary to establish an international crime and international enforcement machinery to avoid recurrence of the Greek tragedy? Probably not in the circumstances, since both the definition of a crime and enforcement authority do seem to be to hand. What is unacceptable and unwise is to treat such a large crime as no crime at all!

6.2 Please Lie to Me!

Our blinkered view of the exercise of governmental authority has many interesting outgrowths. One is the "political question" doctrine in the United States which makes the executive unanswerable to courts in a myriad of situations where political discretion is involved. This is, per se, not wrong, since in proper separation of powers theory courts should not interfere in the exercise of discretion by another branch of government to which this discretion has been allocated. Yet, in separation of power theory, discretion is exercised within legal boundaries, whereas under the political question theory in the United States the executive can choose to disregard international commitments, which are "law of the land", with impunity. This, in a land where you cannot even sell a cup of hot coffee without being sanctioned if the buyer does not know how to handle such dangerous substances!

Another outgrowth of our deference to authority is our tolerance of politicians lying to us. Elections are supposed to be competitions of ideas and competitions of competence, yet they have to a large extent turned into competitions of lying. The key to electoral success is often the ability to reflect the public mood, witness the maddeningly extensive use of pollsters, and to present to us in the most elegant form our own wishes, no matter how unrealistic or dumb. We invite lying in the political process, and we reward the most skilled liars with the highest offices. In the process we lose integrity, original policy definition and conviction politics. It might be argued that politicians are doing democracy's work by playing back to us our own hopes and aspirations, and this would perhaps even be true if our hopes and aspirations were realisable. Alas, often they are not, and we have failed to force politicians to tell us when our dreams cannot be fulfilled.

There is an interesting parallel to private industry in this. In the 19th century train, steel and assorted other barons resorted to stock manipulation without reservation. What they did was to reflect the hopes (and sometimes the fears) of stockholders in their public and not-so-public announcements although they knew that those sentiments were entirely unrealistic. In these cases you could also argue that lying was a part of the process, which was understood and accepted by all participants. Nevertheless, come the 20th century, these practices were outlawed, and nowadays a complex normative system seeks to ensure an extremely high degree of transparency and honesty. Few CEOs of publicly traded companies will dare to share their dreams of their companies' prospects without a solid foundation in fact. Accountability is writ large.

When politicians try to sell their dreams of the country they want to create it is not obvious why they should be able to do so in a more irresponsible way than a CEO selling his smaller dream.

Dreaming is, of course, an important part of politics, and few would want to deny Martin Luther King the right to have and to share a dream. Still, there is a distinction to be made between dreaming and promising. It is OK for Barrack Obama to promote the "Yes, we can" dream, but quite another to let people read your lips saying "no new taxes" as George Bush Senior did, whilst probably knowing that that was a promise he could not keep. It is different to promise to close Guantanamo Bay within a year and to wish for a "green" revolution.

What is more, it is different to betray a promise when you have the means to fulfil it and to enter a compromise when you have no other choice. This does not mean that lying can never be proven, however.

Notwithstanding all the distinctions to be made, and all the caution to be shown, there is no good reason not to punish politicians when they are found to have lied. Most of the distinctions to be made in this case must also be made when judging the behaviour of CEOs, yet we have a well-functioning sanctions system for when they lie and cheat. It is in the public interest to be equally intolerant of the lying and cheating of politicians who are trying to sell us the Tower of London year after year!

As we have seen in the Greek case, one of the problems of outlawing behaviour undertaken under the auspices of government authority is that one political elite is reluctant to punish another for behaviour in which they all habitually engage. This is doubly true for outlawing lying as part of the political process. It is surely not realistic to imagine that this obstacle can be overcome by internationalising the crime in the manner of the International Criminal Court. For this we are too far from Utopia! And even penal provisions similar to those governing the utterances of company officers might go too far, considering the strength of the current paradigm, which assumes that lying will be defeated at the ballot box. The realisation by the public that the ballot box does not keep politics clean, and we have two centuries of proof, should, however, lead to public insistence that political lying becomes illegal in a formal sense. And this realisation should give rise to the creation of an official institution, free of political interference, which, at least, can name and shame offenders. We have an increasing number of non-governmental organisations keeping track of political promises and their fulfilment. That has, no doubt, been a good development. However, what we really need is an official body, something akin to an elections commission, which on behalf of the public can cry foul when the temptation of politicians to feed us our unrealistic dreams becomes too strong.

It is a commonplace to complain that the young generation is indifferent to politics. One reason for this indifference is the perception that politics is all about trickery, partisanship and lying. At least the lying we can do something about!

This does not go to say that the current fad of prosecuting politicians for failed policies is all right. What is going on in Iceland, with the indictment of the premier presiding over the melt-down of the Icelandic financial system, is a witch-hunt by a population which knew very well what was going on, but enjoyed the moment of glory more than it feared the outsized risks taken. Icelanders were foolish—not lied to. What is going on in Hungary, where former government leaders are indicted for failure, and in Ukraine, where a former prime minister was convicted for having signed a natural gas deal, is political persecution pure and simple. These events are all examples of the opposite of good governance, are examples of revenge, intolerance, frustration. Prosecuting politicians for being incompetent is unwise and counterproductive, among other reasons because criminal liability for failure seems to invite a countervailing tolerance of leaders putting their fingers in the till when policies are successful. You cannot outlaw incompetence, you can vote incompetents out of office, but you can and should formally reproach the liars feeding off our naivety and boundless optimism!

6.3 Do not Render unto Caesar

Render unto to Caesar what is Caesar's is good advice. Had popes listened, much letting of blood would have been avoided. And separation of church and state is, indeed, desirable in many other respects. Still, the thinking behind Render unto Caesar has propagated also in undesirable ways. Render unto Caesar has fuelled ideas of absolutism, that we are suffering from even today.

The absolutist monarch ridiculously claimed that his power was derived from God despite the quoted emphatic statement to the contrary in the New Testament. Yet, the propagated God-given nature of absolute power meant that whatever emanated from that power could not be questioned. Hence the monarch was free to abuse his country and his subjects in any way that pleased him.

What is more, other monarchs, with similar claims to power, would logically not question absolute royal rights, since they would then question their own power. As a consequence they would not interfere in the affairs of other monarchs unless it served their own claims of power and authority, and they would never do it by challenging the notion of absolute power. Absolutism was the nursery of the principle of national sovereignty.

As discussed earlier, national sovereignty is not necessarily bad, but has a tendency to obscure central humanitarian imperatives and to make us blind to some of the worst crimes committed.

The conscience of the world rests easily when Robert Mugabe turns the breadbasket of Africa into a hunger state and when the junta of Myanmar creates a nightmare version of communist Albania, just as the world was uninterested in the humanitarian catastrophe created by Mao with his Cultural Revolution and in the killing fields of the Khmer Rouge.

What is more, leaders of too many countries to name thrive on corruption, and in many countries corruption strangles all efforts towards broad based development benefitting the poorest.

Yet, the world conscience rests easily, rests easily on the pillow of national sovereignty. Raping one's own country is not an international crime, and does not impose a duty to protect on other countries.

The sort of responsibility to protect which has been included in resolutions of the Security Council of the United Nations is laudable, but of far lesser reach. There is possibly a consensus emerging that civilian populations must be protected against war crimes, genocide and ethnic cleansing even if it means that other countries must provide this protection. So the Security Council has taken the logical consequence of the Statute of the International Criminal Court and has sought to make sure that war crimes and the like are not only crimes, but can also be prevented. A first step on the path to putting bite into *erga omnes* obligations and a wonderful way of approaching reprehensible behaviour by the two main methods we know from domestic law, that is, criminalisation and prevention. But a first step only!

6.4 If the Individual Would be Subject

It is remarkable that all those who hoist the standard of the individual as society's subject do not apply this view to the construct that is the international community. Kant did not indict national sovereignty as incompatible with the right of the individual to be treated as a subject rather than as an object, and the minimalist state concept of Nozick still has the state as the outer perimeter of his system, although his ultra-individualist perspective would have dictated a world community view rather than a state centric one. Any absolutist element inherent or tolerated in the concept of state should, from the perspective of Kant and Nozick, be declared intolerable, since absolutist powers per definition subjects the citizen to becoming an object.

The missing attack on the absolutist residue contained in the principle of sovereignty is perhaps particularly woeful for Kantians, but it is true to say that no current coherent political science theory puts up any defence for domestic absolutism, and therefore no theory legitimises national sovereignty because it allows rulers a free hand. All defence of sovereignty is premised on self-determination reasoning; mostly wrongheaded democracy rationales, but sometimes based on more palatable 'lesser evil' considerations.

Sovereignty cannot be justified by democracy for the simple reason that few are willing to make the existence of democracy a condition for sovereignty. If this link were made many of the grossest abuse situations would not arise. The current despotism of Mugabe would not subsist in democracy, although it must be acknowledged that in the past democracy in Zimbabwe was incredibly tolerant of the Mugabe descent into outright thuggery.

From a societal design perspective linking sovereignty and democracy is not a complete solution, though, even if it were possible. If sovereignty were only respected by the international community if democracy ruled, sovereignty could still allow minority rights to be violated by a majority. Hitler was, in the first instance, democratically elected!

The lesser evil argument, which argues that sovereignty is the best current organisational principle in the global context, is convincing only if sovereignty is not understood as absolute. Sovereignty is only an adequate concept if abuses of power by the rulers can be stamped out by a vigilant international community. Sovereignty is only defensible if accompanied by behavioural standards enforceable and enforced by the international community.

6.5 Dreaming a Global Charter

The Statute of the International Criminal Court harnesses wonderful embryonic power in the way it has pierced in a most direct manner the protective veil of sovereignty. If one allows oneself to dream what the full being might become, some of our strongest preconceptions must be confronted. We must challenge the notion that commission is so much more reprehensible than omission and that the scale of culpability is determined only by the most directly attributable damage caused by a crime. And we must reject the idea that the international community is a jigsaw puzzle with individual pieces that will independently fit together and form a coherent whole.

The Dutch soldiers at Srebrenica can testify to the perversion of not being allowed to stop an ethnically based massacre, and economists can explain in no uncertain terms how corruption in developing countries is a scourge creating much more damage than most directly inflicted criminal damage. Journalists in many countries can weep so many stories of being harassed and colleagues killed, just because they were telling truth, and of how they felt left alone by the international community despite the strong solidarity between journalists across borders. Most Zimbabweans can scream at their African brethren and the global society and ask how the reign of terror of Robert Mugabe could be allowed, over decades, to turn relative prosperity into absolute destitution.

All this means that we must move towards an international system where we do not take the "official" and "domestic" nature of an act or omission as facts removing the behaviour from legal scrutiny and international sanction. Societal evolution must increasingly make the wielder of governmental authority responsible for acts or omissions that do not correspond to societal expectations and make them accountable to domestic and international courts when transgression occurs. This does not imply that the measure for government action should be perfection, as little as corporate law demands perfection from corporate officers, but in a generation's time we should arrive at a binding set of norms, a Charter if you will, setting out minimum requirements for government actors and establishing an enforcement mechanism similar to that of the Statute of the International Criminal Court.

Chapter 7
A Farewell to Evolution

Abstract Over the past 150 years society has evolved at highest speed in terms of automation, manufacturing efficiency, effective data access and use. In another 50 or 100 years everything will be automated or digitally processed. The role of the human being as a producer will be a thing of the past and its role as decision maker greatly reduced. At such a time the human being will be in an existential conflict with its nature. Humans are born to strive, but when all is taken care of by machines there will be no need to provide—no place for the pursuit of happiness in any material sense. When the tools provided by evolution over millions of years are rendered useless in the space of a few hundred years, how are we going to anchor our existence? Will we experience a new age of spirituality or will a virtual world, indistinguishable from the real one, part us from existence and return our species to original matter?

Keywords Evolution • Darwin • Automation • Manufacturing • Striving • The pursuit of happiness • Virtual reality • Proportionality • Procreation • *Cogito ergo sum* • Original matter

In utterly materialistic times, it is easy to over-prioritize things of substance when contemplating the balance between body and soul. In the criminal law discussions in the first two chapters, this distortion was perhaps not evident, because happiness from a criminal law perspective must necessarily encompass much more than just property and infirmity. Still, even criminal law tends more towards the body than the soul. Whilst it is true that politically incorrect statements, with intended harm to the spirit, can nowadays be criminally sanctioned in a certain number of cases, and that harassment in the work place can end up in court, it does not alter the fact that a slap in the face by a love interest is illegal, but that the much more hurtful verbal put-down is not.

Short of debilitating injury or illness, surely what hurts—and uplifts—us the most, are the attitudes of others towards us, whether these attitudes are expressed verbally or physically. In a perfectly politically correct world one could, of course, imagine a society without hurt, both physical and mental. However, most of us shudder at the thought of a society of anodyne, sanitized social interaction, just

P. Hulsroj, *The Principle of Proportionality*, SpringerBriefs in Law,
DOI: 10.1007/978-94-007-5775-2_7, © The Author(s) 2013

as a Viking might perhaps shudder at the thought of a world without bloodshed. The price we pay for the deepest of sentiments is the risk of hurt. Yet, accepting that the reward outweighs the risk of hurt brings us close to a stand on the classical 19th century utilitarian debate on whether happiness has a qualitative element. John Stuart Mill famously wrote: "It is better to be a human being dissatisfied than a pig satisfied; better to be Socrates dissatisfied than a fool satisfied." It is, however, debatable whether Socrates would have agreed, considering the ultra-nihilism evident in his description of one possible death:

> Now if you suppose that there is no consciousness, but a sleep like the sleep of him who is undisturbed even by the sight of dreams, death will be an unspeakable gain. For if a person were to select the night in which his sleep was undisturbed even by dreams, and were to compare with this the other days and nights of his life, and then were to tell us how many days and nights he had passed in the course of his life better and more pleasantly than this one, I think that any man, I will not say a private man, but even the great king, will not find many such days or nights, when compared with the others.

It is hard to imagine a perspective on happiness less qualitative than that! So utterly in contrast again to Harry Lime in The Third Man:

> … in Italy for 30 years under the Borgias they had warfare, terror, murder, and bloodshed, but they produced Michelangelo, Leonardo da Vinci, and the Renaissance. In Switzerland they had brotherly love—they had 500 years of democracy and peace, and what did that produce? The cuckoo clock.

Suffering as a religion, and much of religion's worship of suffering, is premised on Harry Lime's assumption that pain leads to greatness, that pain releases creative energy. This can be looked at differently, however. It is conceivable that greatness carries with it an inherent risk of suffering, rather than that suffering is the cause of greatness. If greatness is the starting point, it follows that the eternal quest for happiness, so firmly rooted in human evolution, is no spoiler of greatness, but perhaps an enabling cultural attribute, since the hurt that so often accompanies greatness might indeed defeat the great, when not set against an ultimate struggle for happiness. Reduction of misery must not lead to the cuckoo clock.

The societal perspective must always be, however, that society cannot create happiness; it can only create the minimum conditions for happiness. Society's focus is, therefore, on the material, although not exclusively so. The minimum conditions for happiness are also many of the features of modern democratic society: freedom of thought and belief and expression, due process, the right to education. What is interesting is that as our material needs are satisfied increasingly easily, our focus will inevitably become increasingly trained on the non-material. The balance between body and soul will then change. It seems that we are on the verge of a revolution that will question our role as human beings and will force us to redefine what humanness is about.

In 50 or 100 years, bar catastrophe, the role of the human being as a producer will have vanished. The electronic and robotic age will have automated all production, and even decision-making will largely be done electronically. If those who believe that human beings are the mere results of rule-bound acts, and that all human decision-making is only a consequence of cause and effect are actually right, the inescapable conclusion is that all human activity can be captured by electronic means and that all human decision-making can be automated. Everything is relational, everything is a question of proportionality. The intellectual heirs of Professor Singer's animal rights movement, or even machines themselves, will write long tracts on the rights of humanoid computers, accusing the human race not only of speciesism but also of bias towards life lived organically, rather than life lived electronically.

Common sense will be considered to be black magic, because all reasoning can be ultimately captured in zeros and ones and the computers will reason for us. The many surprises rightly or wrongly revealed by "freakonomics" represent, in the final analysis, the rigorous approach to reasoning which the computer will eventually apply. The statistical mining of large data sets from all possible angles will be done as a matter of mechanical course.

The Malthusian constraint will not constrain procreation, because some of the drivers behind procreation will have weakened, such as the need to have many offspring in order to secure one's own old age. Instead, the Malthusian constraint will be a constraint on consumption, and the constraining factor will be natural resources, as we have already begun to experience. In a world in which all production is done automatically, everyone can have a Bentley as long as there is enough Connolly leather. In a transition period, Marx will become relevant again, since capital ownership will be the key to all power when the human being can no longer sell his labour. But capital ownership, too, will lose its lustre when consumption is more than adequate; when it is not the result of achievement or qualification, when it becomes exclusively hereditary, capital ownership will lose its validity and its acceptance. In such a system, most of our values will be turned upside down, our accustomed proportionalities will be maladjusted. The bias will be heavily towards the soul, because the body will be automatically taken care of. The source of pride will not be work and existence will not be defined by the need to provide. Life might become a generalized version of the life of the English landed gentry.

Such a world ultimately poses the question of whether human existence will be sustainable when most of the instincts developed over millions of years of evolution turn out to be useless or even counterproductive—and that in a matter of only a few hundred years.

In the ideal communist society, each individual consumes only what he needs and contributes in accordance with ability. With this construction, Marx avoided the question of the purpose of life when no contribution is needed. Christian religion has not explained what one would do in a Paradise of absolute fulfilment, whereas Buddhist and Hindu religion assumes rebirth until all desire has been eliminated, and the soul has gained perfect peace. Now, using the Buddhist/Hindu tenet of the goal being the elimination of all desire, it would seem that human existence will end not long after man's role as a producer has been made superfluous. If all material needs were fulfilled without effort, if the purpose of life had been eliminated, life itself would become superfluous. The human race would again become original matter.

As mentioned, a German saying has it that "*Der Weg ist das Ziel*". In its wonderful circularity, the phrase leads to the further conclusion that without a destination there can be no journey. Striving for something is the premise on which life is based—the striving for sun, for nutrition, for procreation—and, indeed, it must be assumed that if striving is eliminated then the organism will give up life. Survivors of concentration camps have hauntingly relayed how death crept in when hope disappeared. We must assume that aspiration is the fuel of life. In a roundabout fashion, this realization is the essence of the Faustian bargain: the soul is lost when perfect happiness is attained.

Cynically, one may then conclude that since aspiration is the fuel, it does not matter to what end the aspirations are directed. Marketing is all about creating aspiration independent of product and, in the same fashion, one could suggest that the solution to humankind's future problem of complacency would be the societal marketing of some credible goal or destination towards which humans could direct all their energies. The true desirability of the destination would become a secondary concern. The collective aspiration channelled into Nazism in the 1930s and 1940s shows that this cynicism is not necessarily overblown. It also shows that one of the risks of idleness is that it can be transformed into ideological fanaticism by demagogues. Tempering cynicism, it is probably true to say that there is a qualitative difference in the journey depending on the true desirability of the destination, not necessarily in the dissatisfied sense displayed by Socrates, but in the sense of whether or not the destination has an ennobling function.

When striving was all the rage, the destination, the goal, apart from material wellbeing, was either God or love or both. And both God and love are strong candidates for the human destination when material wellbeing is automatically catered for. Historically, of course, material deprivation has been a strong motivator of religious sentiment, because the hope was that what could not be achieved in the here and now would be achieved in the hereafter. With increases in material prosperity, religious feeling has mostly been on the wane, with one notable exception, that is, in the United States. In The Protestant Ethic and the Spirit of Capitalism, Max Weber sought to explain how materialism and spiritualism can co-exist in the way they do in the United States. Capital accumulation becomes a stepping-stone to Heaven, and although the ascetic element has been thoroughly forgotten in today's United States, it is not overly cynical to suggest that religion in the United States remains an acquisitive tool to win the ultimate prize of eternal life. A contract is entered into with God, according to which you get eternal life in return for behaving well. In this sense, Pascal should have been an American, considering how well his wager fits into this scheme. There is, however, yet another element to calibrate when considering religion as a candidate for the human destination, and that is that people with material wealth and much time on their hands often turn to spiritual themes. When you are well off and have a lot to do you may tend to turn away from religion; when you are well off and have little to do you may have strong reasons to turn to religion, because religion can fill the void. And in an automated world, religion will be one of the few domains that can be safely preserved from the dominance of artificial intelligence, since religion's premise is non-empirical: "Blessed they that have not seen, and yet have believed". Speciesism and the dominance of organic life over electronic life can be justified by religion. Religion as the human destination could become humankind's natural reaction to the superiority of artificial intelligence and the way to finding meaning in an otherwise empty world.

Other time-honoured time-fillers are sports, non-procreational sex and other hobbies. If we again parallelize with the English landed gentry of the past, clearly this type of activity will be the chosen remedy of many, although the not unimportant envy factor will be missing when everyone can devote themselves to the activity of their choice. Like religion, hobbies will be untouched by automation. Hobbies do not have any other aim than emotional and/or physical satisfaction, and the passionate rose grower will surely still want to cut his roses by hand, even if many other gardening tasks can and will be done by machines.

Both religion and hobbies are manifestations of love, and it is therefore perhaps cogent to conclude that in a non-material world, the destination will always be some kind of love (or its mirror image, some kind of hate). Still, love of other human beings merits special consideration. The "Blue Lagoon" species of love with never-ending harmony and unlimited time for togetherness quickly tends to descend into frustration and obsession with one's own navel. If loving another person becomes the sole activity then that love will not live for long. Successful and enduring love tends to serve as a subtext for a life full of other activity, and it is doubtful whether love that is not relational to other aspects of life would even be detectable as love at all. Love might be felt to be absolute in terms of sentiment, but love's precondition might nevertheless be that it needs a canvas of other aspects of life on which it can paint. The Bloomsbury circle would seem to be a frightening example of the fundamental emptiness of life when the overriding preoccupation is describing and experiencing love in all its forms.

In any event, few can spend their lives chronicling love, and this means that even if love becomes the centre of one's life, it must be combined with other pursuits. In fact, a non-material world requires a combination of preoccupations; hobbies might be combined with religion, with the love of other human beings. In an age that, in the final analysis, becomes an age of spirituality, the masses will experience what before was reserved for the few: that life is lived only for its own sake. This sounds nice, but is not easy, because the human being was built for purpose, and most of that purpose will have been eliminated in the non-material world. The proportionality of our value systems will have lost its anchor, and we will be challenged to replace it and to redefine our values relative to the new anchor.

There is a bleaker view of the future. A view that almost takes us into the metaphysics of human existence, *cogito, ergo sum* with a twist, in fact.

No matter where they stand on the nature versus environment debate, most people, as a matter of instinct if nothing else, condition themselves and their social interfaces. The nice apartment seeks to induce a feeling of happiness, the business dinner aims at constructive cooperation. We educate our children by providing for good schools, by means of a carrot-and–stick approach, by making sure that their appearance makes them feel confident. Within the last hundred years, we have added significantly to our repertoire of means of conditioning, however. Aspirin eliminates headaches, silicon eliminates flat chests, Prozac eliminates depression and Viagra eliminates a flagging sex-drive. Genetics have put us at the gates of evolutionary self-service, allowing us to soon eliminate terrible hereditary diseases, but also to design our offspring in much the same way as we choose the colour and extras of a car. And genetics has put a strange sort of immortality within our reach as well, since we are close to being able to clone ourselves ad infinitum. The evolutionary selection mechanism of fitness for purpose may be replaced by evolutionary selection through parental choice. We are conditioned to want to pass on our genes, but soon we might have to adapt to a reality whereby we pass on only those genes we deem desirable, and manipulate those we find undesirable into a more likable state. Turbo-charged evolution or high-speed descent into an evolutionary morass, because we introduce a new relativity of parental preference in the place of the indiscriminate gene-mixing defined by nature's procreational system. A heady cocktail when combined with lives defined by a lack of struggle for survival.

A parallel universe might open up in which we not only choose all the features of our offspring or alter egos, but also, enabled by virtual reality tools and psychopharmacological innovation, one in which we choose our preferred reality, unconstrained by "real reality". The internet obsession, "Second Life", is only a first step in this direction. Of course, story-telling, literature, art, films and television are all creators of virtual reality to some degree, the difference being that one of humankind's possible futures might lead us to take the step fully, so that we can neither physically nor emotionally distinguish between reality and virtual reality. Perhaps the only part of existence we can establish as unambiguously true is "*cogito ergo sum*". Humankind might find a devolutionary path leading to *Selbstaufgabe*, demonstrating that the eventual consequence of biting the apple of knowledge is the irrelevance of human existence as we know it. When sex in the virtual world is so uncomplicated, so liberatingly amoral and yet so deeply emotionally satisfying, why bother with the real thing, particularly if your parents did a poor job of choosing your genes, thereby limiting your choice of potential procreational partners to somebody less attractive than the Angelina Jolie of your virtual world. The virtual world might become much more compelling than opium, with its proven ability to gradually release many a dreamer from his earthly existence.

FSC
www.fsc.org
MIX
Papier aus verantwortungsvollen Quellen
Paper from responsible sources
FSC® C105338

If you have any concerns about our products,
you can contact us on
ProductSafety@springernature.com

In case Publisher is established outside the EU,
the EU authorized representative is:
Springer Nature Customer Service Center GmbH
Europaplatz 3, 69115 Heidelberg, Germany

Printed by Libri Plureos GmbH
in Hamburg, Germany